Baptist Convention of New York
6538 Baptist Way
East Syracuse NY 13057
www.bcnysbc.org

He Loves Me. He Loves Me. He Loves Me.

A Devotional Journal for Every Kind of Day

Authored By BCNY Ministry Wives

Hallelujah!

Give Thanks to the Lord,

For He is good:

His faithful love endures forever.

Psalm 106:1

Acknowledgement

This project would not have been possible without the blessing of the Baptist Convention of New York's Executive Director, Terry M. Robertson. Thank you for believing in and encouraging its completion.

Many thanks are given to the BCNY ministry wives who have willingly submitted devotional entries for this project. You are indeed my heroes. Thank you for sharing your lives with all who will read *He Loves Me. He **Loves** Me. He Loves **Me**.*

All proceeds from this book will be donated to the BCNY Minister's Family Relief Fund.

Kathy Aubrey
BCNY Administrative Assistant

Our Writers

	Devotional on page

Forward

I have done Kelly Minter's study on *Nehemiah* five times. Crazy, right? The book of *Nehemiah* (and Kelly's study of it) has truly rocked my world. There is a phrase found in this Old Testament book that has refined me and my ministry like nothing had ever done before it. The book of Nehemiah records the story of the rebuilding of Jerusalem's crumbled walls as well as Nehemiah's thoughts, prayers, conversations, actions, opposition, and worship. One of his thoughts is what prompted the devotional you hold in your hand.

*After I arrived in Jerusalem and had been there three days, I got up at night, and took a few men with me. I didn't tell anyone **what my God had laid on my heart** to do for Jerusalem.... Nehemiah 2:11-12*

"what God had laid on my heart to do" .... The summer of 2013, God laid on my heart a desire to start working on a devotional. As I prayed about it, He made it clear that it would include writers from the Baptist Convention of New York. Women, like me, who are ministry wives ... ladies who have experienced the same kinds of highs and lows that I have. Women who get it! They have survived (are surviving) the emotional journey of the ministry and of life. Oh how we need to hear from women who have gone through trials and testings, have found God to be faithful in His love, and were willing to be honest enough to share their stories with others.

*I told them how the gracious hand of my God had been on me, and what the king had said to me. They said, "Let's start rebuilding and **they were encouraged to do this good work."** Nehemiah 2:18*

"they were encouraged to do this good work" ... Our desire is that on the pages of this devotional journal, you will find a friend, and you will know that God loves you. Our prayer is that every reader will be encouraged to do the good work God has laid on their heart to do.

Kathy Aubrey

Remember!

"Only be on your guard and diligently watch yourselves, so that you don't forget the things your eyes have seen and so that they don't slip from your mind as long as you live. Teach them to your children and your grandchildren."
Deuteronomy 4:9

The mind can be a slippery place. Somehow I can manage to forget why I opened the refrigerator in the time that it takes to open the door. From conversations that I have had with other women, I know that there's a good chance that you have done the same thing. Of course, there are other things that seem to stick in my mind and refuse to let go. Some of those thoughts are happy memories, and others are hurtful moments that have made themselves at home in my mind. I don't remember making a conscious effort to remember these sticky thoughts, but for some reason they have a tighter grip on my brain.

God tells His people that they must be diligent to make sure that they remember the right things. These are the same people who saw God free them from slavery by striking Egypt with ten terrible plagues. These are the same people who walked on dry ground as the Red Sea stood like walls on each side of them. These are the same people who heard the voice of God thundering on Mount Sinai and begged Him to stop speaking for fear that they would die. Surely these memories must be sticky thoughts, right? How could anyone forget such powerful miracles?

These people would forget what God had done for them. They spent their lives wandering in the wilderness because they didn't believe that God could defeat an army that appeared stronger than their own. If they had remembered God's past faithfulness, they certainly would have trusted Him in future situations. I would love to sit in judgment. I would love to pretend that I could never do such a thing, but I am plagued by the sin of selective forgetfulness as well. Often times, I allow the faithfulness of God to slip right out of my mind.

This is why we must be on guard. God tells us that we must intentionally choose to remember His goodness to us. We must make a point to remember how much He has done for us and how greatly He has blessed us. If we don't, it won't only damage our relationship with Him, but it could also have a negative impact on our children and grandchildren. Even when we don't realize it, we are teaching our children and grandchildren what to remember. We can teach them to choose what they remember based on their emotions, or we can teach them to cling to God's faithfulness and set their eyes on it.

Hannah Attaway has been a ministry wife for 10 years. Her husband is Edwin Attaway, the pastor at First Christian Church in Brushton, NY. They have served there for 4 years, and prior to that they served in ministry in Alabama and Kentucky.

Application

What have you seen God do? How has God blessed you, protected you, and loved you relentlessly? Write these things down. Repeat them to your children and children in your church. Pray that these will be the thoughts that stick.

Reflection: What is God saying to you?

_____

_____

_____

_____

_____

_____

_____

_____

_____

_____

_____

_____

_____

_____

_____

Remind your Heart

"Take care lest your heart be deceived, and you turn aside and serve other gods and worship them;"
Deuteronomy 11:16

Have you ever noticed how easily our hearts are deceived? How the slightest change in our circumstances or emotions can shake the very confidence of our faith?

On a hot summer day in August of 2007, with my knees covered in dirt, my face in the ground, and in the embrace of my husband, I watched my then 27 years of life being buried into a grave. As my mother's coffin began to make its way down into a six foot ditch, my heart began its course to a place even darker than that tomb, where for a brief instance it knew of no love and for that moment in time my pain became my god. I remember as those minutes progressed they seemed like years, as dirt filled up the hole where I felt my heart was left, but then something happened…as I wept in my grief, I remember letting out a cry and said "I still love you Lord." I know that cry was not because I did at the moment, but because somehow my heart knew that He STILL loved me even then. In the midst of my suffering and my pain, in what has been the hardest trial of my life, I had to remind my heart of God's love for me…lest it were deceived.

There's something about God's love that we don't quite understand, something that our finite minds cannot completely grasp, and something that we lost back when it was all perfect. You see, our hearts were deceived a long long time ago and it was then where we began to doubt the love of our father; a steadfast, immovable, unshakeable, perfect love. Just as this generation of Israelites in Deuteronomy 11, our hearts also need to be reminded of God's love; of His "greatness and mighty hand" (v2 - *"consider the discipline of the Lord your God, His greatness, mighty hand, and outstretched arm"*) in our times of affliction, of His provision and faithfulness in the wilderness of our lives (v5- *"and what He did to you in the wilderness until you came to this place",*) and of His promises and grace as we look toward the promise land (v12- *"a land that the Lord your God cares for. The eyes of the Lord your God are always upon it..."*) Oh how he loves us!

In our journey there will be valleys, droughts, and famines, and in those times we must take care of our hearts lest they be deceived…Our obedience + His love = Strength for the road. In our afflictions, in our sufferings, and in our trials, let us always remind our hearts of this truth, HE HAS LOVED US TO DEATH!

"But God shows his love for us in that while we were still sinners, Christ died for us." Romans 5:8

Heledy Rymer and her husband, William, are the Marriage and Family Ministry leaders at Christ Crucified Fellowship in Manhattan. Heledy has been a ministry wife for two years serving as core team members of this church plant.

Application

Has there been that moment in your life when even though circumstances felt differently, you knew God still loved you?

_____

_____

_____

_____

_____

Reflection: What is God saying to you?

_____

_____

_____

_____

_____

_____

_____

_____

_____

_____

_____

_____

_____

_____

Frozen Fog

"I will never leave you or forsake you."
Deuteronomy 31:6b

Have you ever heard of such a thing? Frozen fog I mean. Well that is what the weather guy called it anyway. When the sun hit the tips of the trees on the edge of the horizon this morning, I had to set my cup of coffee down and just gaze with my mouth wide open at the sight. The pink sky shone as a backdrop to the sparkling vegetation. The branches glistened with silver light all along my path as I drove to work. It was so beautiful I began praising God through tearing eyes, thanking him for the privilege of experiencing God's creation at one of its finest moments. I turned onto the main road, still amazed at the beauty and began the descent into the valley.

All too quickly the view I had been enjoying passed and I was faced with a sea of clouds, fog so dense it was impossible to see far down the road. The way became slow and hazardous and the reminder of the bleakness of winter began to set in. Just as the gloom was beginning to penetrate my spirit as well, the sun burst through the curtain that had blocked my path. Brilliance reappeared! It was at that moment I was reminded (loud and clear!) that my travel through life was exactly like the road to work this morning. It is always filled with God's presence even when I am unaware of it. His love endures the bleakest of times. Some days are brilliant, some are foggy.

Some are so amazingly Christ centered and some feel like I will live in doom forever. But the promise of the sun (Son) reappearing is always there, to give me hope, to direct my path, to give me vision. His love will always burn through the fog and be my navigator. Just as it did this morning.

Fog

The evening fog falls heavy on squinting eyelids.

My neck strains to catch a glimpse of what lies ahead yet is hidden.

"For I know the plans I have for you" says the Lord..

But the fog remains thick.

The steamy jungle-like path ahead allows for limited view.

When will a clearing appear? When will the fog lift?

For now it seems the focus must be on a portion of the mist closest to me, one drop of moisture on the leaf before my eyes.

Reflected in this droplet is a life time of love. It is all I need to step forward. Guide me, O Lord.

Kathy Ray has been a ministry wife for over 20 years. Her husband Don is Associate Pastor at Pleasant Valley Baptist Church in Geneseo NY.

Application

Have you experienced a "frozen fog" in your walk with the Lord?

_____

_____

Reflection: What is God saying to you?

_____

_____

_____

_____

_____

_____

_____

Because He Loves Me

They refused to listen and did not remember Your wonders
You performed among them. They became stiff-necked and
appointed a leader to return to their slavery in Egypt.
But You are a forgiving God, gracious and compassionate,
slow to anger and rich in faithful love, and You did not
abandon them. Even after they had cast an image of a calf
for themselves and said, "This is your God who brought
you out of Egypt," and they had committed terrible
blasphemies,
Nehemiah 9:17-18

Because He loves us, God is ready to pardon us when we are disobedient. Because He loves us, God will direct, protect and guide us in the way we should go in spite of our disobedience, rebellion and hardness of heart. Because He loves us, even when we do not remember what all God has done for us, not remembering his capabilities because he is limitless. Praise Be to God!

I heard him calling me while I was deep in sin, as he called to Adam and Eve in the garden when they hid in their sin because they were naked. God already knew where they were, but he called out to them asking, "Where are you?" The Lord our God calls out to us and gives us a chance to tell the truth and repent. No matter how far or deep we are in our sins, we can always turn back to God with repentance and obedience.

Also, to show God our sorrow for sinning, we too can fast and pray just like the children of Israel and confess our sins. How soon we forget all of the great things our God has done for us. Even sometimes returning to the sin we were forgiven of or delivered from. We grow accustomed to those things that so easily beset us. This is what they refer to as "stinkin' thinkin'." Imagine helping someone and they repeat the same thing over and over again. At some point man would stop helping, but God doesn't. Thank you Lord for showing mercy on us and sparing us from those things we deserve, but do not get. When we go with our plans and not be obedient to God, he still loves us in spite of ourselves. He is a gracious and a forgiving God. No matter what you do or have done, God is forgiving and compassionate toward you if you will only repent with a sincere heart.

As we've read in verse 18, the molten calf the Israelites made, they gave all the credit for their freedom from Egypt to something tangible that has no power, cannot feel, hear or see, nor answer the prayers that would be lifted up. What things have we done that were offensive to God? How many times do we make other things or people our god and give full credit to them instead of God? Is your work your god, how about your car? Perhaps your money, which its purpose is used for purchases and service. All of these are already His; He is just letting us borrow, use or have access to them.

It is important for us to tell the story to our children what God has done for us. Or to anyone who will listen. Also we must mention what will happen if we are disobedient to Him so the pattern(s) of sin are not repeated. *But You are a forgiving God, gracious and compassionate slow to anger and rich in faithful love, and You did not abandon them.*

Denise Robinson has been a ministry wife for 15 years. She and her husband/pastor, Brian, have been at Fillmore Community Church in Buffalo NY for 3½ years.

Application

Have you experience God's gracious and compassionate character? Briefly tell how.

_____

_____

Reflection: What is God saying to you?

A Shield Around Me

"But you are a shield around me, O Lord; you bestow glory on me and lift up my head. To the Lord I cry aloud, and He answers me from His holy hill."
Psalm 3:3-4

Have you ever been in a situation where you actually "felt" the Lord's presence around you, protecting you from something or someone? Like maybe when you should have been in a car accident, but miraculously, it did not happen? I have read stories where people have said they saw heavenly beings surrounding someone, protecting them from danger.

'Jesus loves me this I know, for the Bible tells me so." Most of us have probably sung this our entire lives and we know it is true. But do we really KNOW it. I have believed this my entire life but there was a time when Jesus made His love known to me in a very personal way. It began when one of my daughters was born and was even more evident when she died. Dana was born with several birth defects, the most prominent being her left ear was not formed correctly. I knew that my God was the God of miracles and so I prayed and prayed and prayed that I would wake up one morning and her ear and other issues would be made perfect. After a while, when it was obvious that He was not going to answer that prayer the way I wanted it answered, I cried out to Him. I felt His arms around me telling me that He loved me and He loved Dana and He was in control. I was to trust in Him. And with that shield around me, I was able to let it go. Dana was a beautiful, well-adjusted child who did not let her physical deformity affect her ability to live her life to the fullest. She had about 10 surgeries to correct her issues, beginning when she was 5 years old. I believe she felt God's shield around her as she endured these surgeries and came out stronger. She became a cheerleader in high school and valedictorian of her class. I will never know what happened that made her decide that suicide was her only option. But I have never felt God's shield around me as I did at that time.

I don't remember much about that first year. I do remember that I could not pray. The words just would not come. I knew God was there. I cried out to him constantly, but I was empty. Looking back on that time, I know that God was the shield around me. I lived the "Footprints" poem. God carried me. He held me up. He loved me regardless of my actions and feelings. Because I believe God's Word, because I believe Psalm 3:3-4, I believe that God was there with my daughter at her darkest hour. Why does it seem that God intervenes sometimes and sometimes He doesn't? Why does it seem like God answers some prayers and not others (in the way we would like them answered)? I used to wish I had the answer to those questions. But you know, it really doesn't matter. I believe in God, I believe He loves me and He is my shield. I either believe or I don't. I trust or I don't.

How many times do we feel unloved or unlovable? But we can KNOW that God loves us, that He is there all the time. He is waiting on us to turn to Him. He wants us to cry out to Him, to tell Him our problems, our hurts. He wants to love on us. Nothing is too small to take to God. He wants to bestow His glory on us.

Linda Sallis has been a ministry wife for 34 years. Her husband, Steve Sallis, has been on church staff, has been a pastor, and now he is the Church Growth Assistant at the Baptist Convention of New York. Linda has served faithfully by his side.

Application

Have you felt God's shield around you?

_____

_____

_____

_____

_____

Reflection: What is God saying to you?

_____

_____

_____

_____

_____

_____

_____

Because I am His Child

The LORD hath heard my supplication:
the LORD will receive my prayer."
Psalm 6:9

I was at my daughter's house in Texas awaiting the arrival of our first grandchild, when the phone rang one morning. I was surprised that it was my sister calling from Illinois. I remember her calm voice tell me she had some bad news. The next thing I remember I was sitting in the floor holding the phone to my ear and crying.

Her son, just two years younger than I, had been diagnosed with Acute Myelogenous Leukemia. The doctors told him it was in an advanced stage and that his prognosis was only a few weeks of life left. He was 37 years old.

I did what I always do during a crisis….I PRAYED. No one had to remind me to pray. I didn't have to write David's name on a list somewhere so I wouldn't forget to call his name in prayer. I prayed when I first woke up; I prayed all through the day; I prayed at night before I went to bed. For the first time in my life I prayed "without ceasing" (I Thessalonians 5:17). I asked everyone I knew to pray for this brother-nephew of mine. My heart was breaking.

David and I grew up in the same house or right next door to each other. We were more like siblings than nephew and aunt. I remember when I went to kindergarten and my mother was asked if I were the oldest or only child in the family in school. My mom said I was the only child, to which I explained that while that was true the next year I'd be the oldest because David would be in school. My mom replied that David was not my brother. "Well who is he??" I cried! I knew he called my sister "Mommy" and my mom "Grandma" but I'd never realized he wasn't my brother until then. And now, that brother-nephew was sick unto death and there didn't seem to be anything I could do about it. I prayed.

I tried to pray "Thy will be done," but the words stuck in my throat. What if it were God's will to take David to Heaven? What if it were God's will for him to suffer a horrible death? What if it weren't God's will to heal him completely? I cried.

One day I was reading in Philippians. It seems Paul had a good friend name Epaphroditus. They were like brothers, and he had been sick – "unto death" (Philippians 2:27), but Paul said, "but God had mercy on him; and not on him only, but on me also, lest I should have sorrow upon sorrow." Those words jumped off the page at me. God understood how much I loved David. He understood I would have "sorrow upon sorrow" if David died, and BECAUSE GOD LOVES ME, because I AM HIS CHILD, he wants to give me my HEART'S DESIRE (Psalm 37:4). It didn't do any good to try to pray pious prayers of "Thy will be done" when in my heart I wanted David healthy and strong again. God knew my heart and He loved me. My prayers changed.

It occurred to me maybe I was afraid to pray for healing. Maybe I didn't really believe God could do it. All the doctors said it was hopeless. So I began to pray differently. I began to pray, "Because I'm Your child and You love me, I ask you to HEAL David." I prayed this prayer without ceasing for months…years even….

David retired from coaching high school football a few years ago when he turned 63! ☺ Today, he and his wife travel around the United States in their RV.

Did my prayers heal David? Absolutely NOT! God healed David. Was it God's will to heal David all along? Possibly. Did it grow my faith? All I know is, when I'm faced with a mountain now, it's comforting to climb up in my Father's lap and say, "Daddy, because You love me so much, will you help me please?"

And He always does.

Lyn Hart is a ministry wife with 49 years of experience. She served as a pastor's wife for 32 years then as a Director of Missions wife for 17 years, - where she currently serves. Her husband, Ed Hart, is the Central New York Baptist Association Director of Missions.

Application

Have you ever struggled (or are you struggling now) with praying 'They will be done?"

_____

_____

_____

_____

_____

_____

Reflection: What is God saying to you?

_____

_____

_____

_____

_____

_____

_____

_____

_____

_____

_____

_____

_____

Get A Strong Hold On Jesus

The Lord is a refuge for the oppressed, a stronghold in times of trouble. Those who know your name will trust in you, for you, Lord, have never forsaken those who seek you.
Psalm 9:9-10

Life is tough, full of challenges, and for me, circumstances seem to be getting harder to cope with by the day. My schedule, no matter how well I plan, is filled with countless interruptions and a pattern of seemingly insurmountable obstacles. My foster children and adopted children who came from difficult backgrounds always present unexpected experiences to my household. My mom who is blind needs my help and support every day. I work alongside my husband helping many people with their problems. Frustration, confusion, heavy burdens and unpredictable troubles frequently weigh me down.

Webster's Dictionary gives the definition for oppression as "physical or mental distress." To oppress is to "weigh heavily on the mind, spirits or senses, or keep one down by the cruel or unjust use of authority."

Oppression is a carefully directed tool of the enemy, the devil, to turn me away from the good direction that God has me headed in. Oppression discourages, produces high frustration levels, puts me in a depressed state and keeps me from functioning in God's peace and clarity. It enters my heart, mind, will and emotions and can effectively stop my productivity. I know I am not alone; many people today are overcome by the oppression of Satan, the deceiver who "keeps us down by his cruel and unjust use of authority."

The definition of refuge is a "shelter or protection from danger." The Lord uses the word in Scripture to describe a spiritual place I can run to for His comfort, peace, help, strength, encouragement and blessings in the midst of a storm, battle or trouble of any kind.

In the middle of the troubles and hustle and bustle of life, God has a plan to rid me of the ugly symptoms of oppression and get me back on track with His agenda. In 1 John 4:4, I find great encouragement, hope and promise, *You are of God, little children, and have overcome them, because He who is in you is greater than he (Satan) who is in the world.* My Heavenly Father does not want me to be overcome by the enemy's tactics. God is greater than all the trials that come to my life.

I can have spiritual victory if I do things God's way. I have learned to run to the Lord as my refuge and strength in times of trouble. When I read God's Word I exchange the devil's stronghold for God's words of truth. I ask Him to show me the steps He wants me to take. Psalm 32:8 says, *I will instruct you and teach you in the way you should go; I will guide you with My eye.* The Lord is always with me, watching me, willing to help me and teach me. As He speaks to me, it is my responsibility to listen to His directions and to obey Him.

Like the psalmist, I can get a stronghold on God's truth, *Those who know your name will trust in you, for you, Lord, have never forsaken those who seek you.* I must obey God by seeking His answers through His Word to me. As I look to Him for answers and guidance, I fully trust and believe He will not leave or forget me. He really cares about all the troubles that come my way.

I trust God as I speak to Him in prayer. Philippians 4:6-7 says, *Be anxious for nothing, but in everything by prayer and supplication, with thanksgiving, let your requests be made known to God; and the peace of God, which surpasses all understanding, will guard your hearts and minds through Christ Jesus.* I desperately need His peace in all of my troubles. As I share my heavy burdens with Him in prayer, I take time to give Him thanks for the problem, for His plan for me and for His answer. I thank Him that He will *work all things out for good* (Romans

8:28) as I trust Him, listen to His leading and obey His directions. Being filled with thanksgiving through all of life's messes has brought me the wonderful peace of God.

When troubles come, the real answer is to take time to put God first, to spend quality time in His Word and to listen to what He says. He made us, He knows every struggle we face and He sent His one and only Son Jesus to die for our sins. Jesus knows about all of our troubles and came to lift us up, strengthen us and give us hope. The trial may not be removed, but His desire is to bring peace and victory over oppression. Jesus loves us, is always faithful and keeps His promises in whatever problems come our way.

We must take time to:
1. Make God our first priority
2. Seek God's direction from His Word
3. Believe God's promises that never fail
4. Pray and give thanks to God
5. Obey God daily

Dear Heavenly Father,

When troubles come my way, help me to run to you as my refuge, shelter and protection. When oppression takes over my mind, will and emotions, give me strength to trust You and believe that You will never leave me or let me down. Give me victory in getting a strong hold on You, my hope, helper, strength and comfort. Help me to hold onto your Word through every trial and trouble.

In Jesus' name, Amen

Elaine O'Neill has been married to her husband, Dennis, for 33 years. Together they have served at Living Gospel Baptist Church in Rutherford, New Jersey, where Dennis is the pastor.

Application

What obstacles are you facing? Finances, family troubles, relationships, illness, rebellious children, job related problems or other challenges can weigh you down. Is the devil making you feel defeated and oppressed leaving you paralyzed? Run to the Lord, get a strong hold on Jesus, trust Him and believe His Word.

Reflection: What is God saying to you?

_____

_____

_____

_____

_____

_____

_____

_____

_____

_____

_____

_____

I Am Confident

I am still confident of this: I will see the goodness of the Lord in the land of the living. Wait for the Lord; be strong and take heart and wait for the Lord.
Psalm 27:13-14

Everyday struggles are hard. We face many things, some harder than others. Some are very painful, both physical and emotional. Christ tells us that He faced so much more and understands what we are going through.

Be confident that we will see the goodness of the Lord. Know that even when we feel that we have lost a battle the Lord has already won the war.

We need to wait, be patient, be still and know that He is God! (Psalm 46:10). Our strength is found in Him. (Psalm 46:1)

God's timing is perfect. When our confidence is based in Christ our lives are less stressful, not easier, just less stressful.

He knows my past and yet...He still is willing to be in my present and hold my future!

He knows my present and yet...He is willing to forgive my past and secure my future!

He knows my future and yet...He has thrown my past sins as far as the east is from the west and carries me through the present!

Lorraine Goewey has been a ministry wife for 17 years. Her husband, Dan, was the pastor at Grace Baptist Church in Rome NY for ten and a half years.

Application

Do you find it difficult sometimes to be confident that you will see the goodness of the Lord? In what area are the most vulnerable to doubt?

_____

_____

_____

Reflection: What is God saying to you?

He Is My Everything

*Blessed is the one whose transgression is forgiven, whose
sin is covered. Blessed is the man against whom the Lord
counts no iniquity, and in whose spirit there is no deceit.*
Psalm 32:1-2

It's amazing to consider Jesus' upside down
kingdom and just how different it is from the worlds! Here
the psalmist proclaims that those who have been forgiven
of sin are "blessed" whereas in the world, it's often times
the practice of sin for one's own personal advancement that
is of great gain.

Throughout my walk as a disciple of Jesus, this has
been a means of warfare that I always have had to engage
in; the conscious fight to believe that my worth, identity
and strength comes from the fact that my transgressions
have been forgiven and my iniquities are no more because
of the once and for all sacrifice made on my behalf by my
Lord.

When I fail to remember this truth, I tend to become
less secure in my adoption as a child of the Risen King and
more likely to act as though I have to *earn* His love and
attention. If I am honest, this is probably most vividly

demonstrated in my prayer life. Guilt ridden by my sin, I come before the Father as though He would turn me away should I not use the most eloquent of words. I also become fixed upon my works as opposed to gazing upon His finished work on the cross. Not to mention, the tendency to place my hope in something temporal like a job title or a relationship.

Oh, but when I contemplate on the good news of the gospel! I am anchored by the hope that while still a wretched sinner, I am loved and pursued by Christ, beyond my ability to fully comprehend. No longer defined by my iniquity but clothed in the perfect righteousness of Jesus Christ. These foundational truths move me from a place of a downward spiral of introspection to a posture of praise.

That my Savior would leave His riches in heaven including the ongoing praise of innumerable angels to clothe Himself in humanity, living a life I could never, and dying the death I should have - just to give me a gift I didn't deserve, truly I am blessed.

So I will venture to wage war against the lies and misconceptions I am most vulnerable to and live in the grace extended to me each day. I will fight to enjoy the love He has for me, free from having to earn it because more than two thousand years ago, my Redeemer said it best, *"It is finished."*

 Shanika Hart has been a ministry wife for nearly a year. Her husband Kenneth is church planter/pastor at Christ Crucified Fellowship in Washington Heights in New York City.

Application /Prayer

Father, thank You for the forgiveness offered to me through the cross of Christ and that my sin is separated from me as far as the East is from the West. I thank you because You saw fit to send Jesus to accomplish for me, what I could never on my own strength. I ask for Your forgiveness when I forget this truth and choose to believe that I have to be my own savior, hoping in my accomplishments and despairing in my disappointments. Would you help me to apply the gospel in every area of my life so that whether I am abased or I abound, my joy will consistency be found in You alone. In Jesus' name, Amen.

Reflection: What is God saying to you?

When I Am Fearful

I sought the Lord, and He answered me and delivered me from all my fears. Those who look to Him are radiant with joy; their faces will never be ashamed.
Psalm 34:4-5

Walking the streets of my hometown alone, scared, and shamed, I asked the question that so many of us ask, why me Lord? I talked to God often but usually only in times of trouble and confusion. The Lord answered me that day. I was a sinner and deserved every heart ache and every pain the world had to offer. He spoke to me through His word, the only scripture that I had memorized, John 3:16 *For God so loved the world that He gave His only begotten Son, that whoever believes in Him should not perish but have everlasting life.* I had just found out that I was pregnant. I was seventeen, single, and scared. I sought God that day as never before. I praised God that I was not alone and that with Him I could handle anything.

A few years earlier I received the Lord as my savior. I attended a youth group meeting with a friend from school and heard the Gospel message. I had never heard the gospel presented so personally before and I know that was the day that I became God's child. My life was changed on the inside but no one else could tell! I started talking (praying) to my Lord and Savior from that day forward but that was all. I believe I started my spiritual journey that day.

I had a crisis of faith. I believed I had a friend in Jesus but I didn't even know what I really had. I had not realized what an awesome God I believed in. I walked the streets that day but not alone. I believed that day that I could handle anything this world could give. With the love of Christ, I was not alone. It was this crisis in my life that made me realize that God was waiting for me to finally understand that I was His and I was not alone. God loved me, a sinner.

My walk with the Lord may have started at a youth meeting a few years earlier; but my journey with my Savior started that day, as I knew He walked with me. "I sought the Lord and He heard me, and delivered me from all my fears. They looked to Him and were radiant, and their faces were not ashamed." Psalm 34:4-5

- **I sought** God, and my desperate cry was heard. He loves to hear our cry of pain and despair. He is a God who loves sinners, broken and lost.
- **He hears** our prayers and answers with what we need, not always what we want!
- **He delivers** us from all our fears with a peace and love that only He can provide.
- **Look** and seek a friendship with Him and you will never be alone.
- God's beauty will make you **radiant**. You will be transformed.
- I will not be **ashamed**. I am a forgiven sinner. God has given me His love and peace.

I am in awe of my Savior every day. I am still on a journey, and what a journey it has been. That seventeen year old girl still walks and talks to God. She still has crises in her life and her Lord and Savior is still right beside her. His love has carried her and will continue to carry her through all circumstances.

My talks with God are the whole of my day not just when I am in despair. I now praise God for all the troubles in my life that draw me closer to Him. I praise Him for the joys in my life that draw me closer to Him. What an awesome God we serve. I am still amazed that with just a word, God answers us. He knows me, and loves me and answers my questioning heart with just a word, a verse, a song when I need it most.

He loves me!

 Judy Downey has worked in many areas of church work since 1980, but has been a ministry wife for 9 years. Her husband, Dave, has served as minister of music first and now pastor at Adirondack Community Church in Newton Falls, NY.

Application

Have you ever been alone, ashamed, or scared? Are you now? Seek the Lord ... tell Him about it and let Him deliver you.

_____

_____

_____

_____

Reflection: What is God saying to you?

Even When My Heart is Broken

The Lord is near the brokenhearted; He saves those
crushed in spirit. Many adversities come to the one who is
righteous, but the Lord delivers him from them all.

Psalm 34:18-19

"Linda!...Linda!" I could hear the anguish in my Dad's voice. It was Sunday morning and I had slipped out of the Worship Service to call him after noticing there was a missed call from him on my phone. I couldn't imagine why he would be calling me during the church service. "Yes, Papa" I replied, my concern growing more and more with every second. Could something have happened to my brother...to one of my aunts or an uncle...? "It's Mama...she passed away last night." Never once, in those fleeting seconds, did I think he would be telling me that it was my Mom who had died. I had just talked with her the night before...actually I talked with her every day! We had such a close relationship, friends as much as mother and daughter. Overall, at age 71, she was in good health. My Dad cried and though I felt like I could barely breathe, I tried to comfort him. He was in Virginia, and I was nearly

500 miles away in New York. I felt so helpless, so alone, and so brokenhearted.

I didn't allow myself to cry, though I wanted to scream and wail. My husband, Charlie, was still preaching. After returning to the sanctuary, I was able to communicate to him that we needed to leave. I just couldn't bring myself to the point that I was able to tell him why. He came to me as I sat on the front row, head bowed, "Is it my Mom?" he asked. She was 83 and in poor health; I shook my head, "no". Next, to my amazement, he asked, "Is it your Mom?" I nodded my head "yes". "Did she die?" As I had to acknowledge this fact, the tears began to flow freely. My church family gathered around me and comforted me and prayed over me. I really don't like to show my emotions, but, I believe that God knew I would need all of my brothers and sisters around me at that moment. It was like God himself was reaching down and embracing me and loving me.

The Lord is near to the brokenhearted
And saves those who are crushed in spirit. (Psalm 34:18)

What a wonderful promise! The Lord, the one true God, is near to the brokenhearted. Think about it, it's when our hearts are broken that we feel the most alone. We start feeling that God doesn't love us or that He has forsaken us. We question why God would allow such a thing to happen. God wants each of us to know that no matter what the circumstance, whether our broken heart resulted from mistakes we made or because of something we had no control over, He is near! "The Lord is near to all who call upon Him, to all who call upon Him in truth." (Psalm 145:18). Call on the Lord when your heart is broken, He is near! God "saves those who are crushed in spirit". He rescues and heals those who are surrendered to Him. "He heals the brokenhearted and binds up their wounds". (Psalm 147:3). Have you ever seen a scar from a wound that should have had stitches, but didn't? The wound is healed but the scar is rough and jagged. We have a beautiful picture, in Psalm 147, of our Savior binding a wound to bring proper healing. Oh how He loves us!

Many are the afflictions of the righteous,
But the Lord delivers him out of them all. Psalm 34:19

Many...oh, let's just stop and camp here for a moment. Many, not few or rare or infrequent, but "many are the afflictions of the righteous". (I was tempted to put an exclamation point here.) Yet, a lot of folks think the Christian life should be easy. How many times have I heard, "I'm too blessed to be stressed"? And let's face it; there aren't many prayer requests at the Wednesday night prayer meeting for more afflictions! But, should there be? The Psalmist declared, "It is good for me that I was afflicted, that I might learn your statutes". (Psalm 119:71). We want to be included among the righteous, but not at the cost of suffering. God can use afflictions to transform us into the people He wants us to be. James said, "My brethren, count it all joy when you fall into various trials, knowing that the testing of your faith produces patience. But let patience have *its* perfect work, that you may be perfect and complete, lacking nothing". (James 1:2-4) Paul told the Romans, "...we also glory in tribulations, knowing that tribulation produces perseverance; and perseverance, character; and character, hope. Now hope does not disappoint, because the love of God has been poured out in our hearts by the Holy Spirit who was given to us". (Romans 5:3-5). That's a beautiful picture; the love of God being poured into our hearts by the Holy Spirit.

Being a follower of Jesus Christ has never meant a life free from problems. If you find that you don't have trials, perhaps in light of scripture, you should re-evaluate your spiritual life. Jesus told His disciples, "In the world you have tribulation, but take courage; I have overcome the world." (John 16:33b). His betrayal and crucifixion was approaching and He was preparing them for the tribulation to come. They understood that through their faith in Him, they would overcome also. The victories that we experience today don't happen because we are such fine folks. Our victories are because of our faith in Jesus Christ. I am reminded of what Paul said in Galatians 2:20, "I have been crucified with Christ; and it is no longer I who live, but Christ lives in me; and the *life* which I now live in the flesh, I live by faith in the Son of God, who loved me and gave Himself up for me."

God is faithful and He promises that although our afflictions are many, He will deliver us from them <u>all</u>! How wonderful to realize that we don't have to struggle, trying to overcome afflictions on our own. As our faith in God is strengthened, it becomes easier to fully rely on Him to see us through any situation, any affliction, any broken heart.

Linda Evans ministers with her husband/pastor, Charles Evans, at Park Slope Community Church in Brooklyn, New York. They have ministered there for 16 years. Linda also serves on the Executive Board of the Baptist Convention of New York.

Application

Is your heart broken? Call out to God.

_____

_____

_____

_____

Reflection: What is God saying to you?

_____

_____

_____

_____

_____

_____

_____

_____

Patiently Waiting

I waited patiently for the LORD; He turned to me and heard
my cry. He lifted me out of the slimy pit, out of the
mud and mire; he set my feet on a rock and gave me a firm
place to stand. He put a new song in my mouth,
a hymn of praise to our God.
Many will see and fear the LORD and put their trust in him.
Psalm 40:1-3

Have you ever experienced waiting for a long period of time that you actually cried because the wait was too hard and long? I remember one incident that happened to me during the severe snow storm in the tri-state area last October. I was stuck in my car, only 2 miles away from home, for more than 2 hours – then when I got to my street, I wasn't allowed to drive or walk onto it because of the fallen trees and wires dangling all over. Feelings of frustration and fear flooded my whole being while I was stranded in the middle of the road... waiting. Waiting for the storm to pass and not knowing what was going to happen or where I would spend my night made me vulnerable. Tears were my only outlet that allowed me to keep on waiting.

Isn't this so much like our lives here on this world? We await the final judgment and the final comfort for the pain and suffering we are currently experiencing. While waiting, we are continuously facing life's turmoil – and as Titus 2:13 declares "while we wait for the blessed hope—the appearing of the glory of our great God and Savior, Jesus Christ," we wait with anticipation for the second coming of the LORD with the hope that sustains us through the wait – and we are told by the Psalmist to wait patiently for the LORD.

To be patient while we are waiting is not that easy. The Bible has about 28 verses that mention the words "patient" or "patiently." Out of these verses, most of them are connected to waiting upon the LORD. We are told to be patient in waiting, in facing afflictions, in listening to God and in relating to fellow believers. Being patient means that we do not fret or whine or complain while we wait – but rather seek Him and cling to Him in His silence, this requires faith in Him. Not being patient is usually the result of pride and sometimes the LORD gives us life experiences that would humble us and teach us patience.

To wait patiently is one of the hardest lessons in our spiritual journey; but it promises to make us strong in the Lord. According to Philippians 3:8 "What is more, I consider everything a loss because of the surpassing worth of knowing Christ Jesus my Lord, for whose sake I have lost all things. I consider them garbage that I may gain Christ." Knowing that without Christ, everything we have is "dung" or garbage and we do not deserve anything. This allows us to have a proper perspective about His grace and His mercy upon us; so even if we deserve worse we claim His goodness and wait for the best in our lives.

While waiting we should always remember that God loves us and wants to give us a fulfilling life. John 10:10 states "I have come that they may have life, and have it to the full." In Jeremiah 29:11, "For I know the plans I have for you," declares the LORD, "plans to prosper you and not to harm you, plans to give you hope and a future," we know He has a plan for our lives…and we need to wait patiently as His plans for us would come to pass.

Psalm 40:1-3 reminded me of a milestone in my life when I chose to obey the Lord and break up my engagement with my ex-fiancé. Those heartbroken days of waiting upon the Lord to see how He would unfold His will through that painful experience, was the loneliest period of my life. One of those lonely nights while crying myself to sleep, I would claim this verse "I waited patiently upon the Lord and He heard my cry …" and then I felt like God reached down and embraced me allowing me to feel complete in Him. That moment was a turning point in my waiting upon the LORD. I was being "lifted out of the slimy pit..." Not only did I sleep well that night, but the LORD also "gave me a place to stand and set my feet upon the rock". To this day, that experience enabled me to help a lot of women who are going through heartbroken experiences and also allowed me to minister to women who are waiting for God's best in their lives. And just as verse 3 states, "he puts a new song in my mouth...many will see and fear the Lord and put their trust in him" through all the pains and waiting patiently for God's best in my own life, other people are being led to trust in the LORD.

The Bible is filled with heroes of faith going through waiting; Abraham who waited until his old age to have his son Isaac; Jacob who waited for 7 more years to have Rachel; Elijah waited for the Lord to send rain. Joseph waited upon the LORD in prison. The Israelites waited upon the LORD in different periods of their nation's growth, and in the New Testament we have one example of a man in John 5:1-15 that waited for 30 years until Jesus came along and healed him. All these Biblical stories are recorded to give us encouragement as we continue on "waiting patiently" upon the LORD – until He would hear our cry.

Florence Co is the minister of Worship and Music at Bible Church International in Randolph, NJ. She has served there for 11 years.

Application

Are you waiting for something? Has it brought you to tears? Can you believe God will hear your cry, and renew your soul?

_____

_____

Reflection: What is God saying to you?

_____

_____

_____

_____

_____

_____

_____

Casting Our Burdens

Cast your burden on the LORD, and He will sustain you;
He will never allow the righteous to be shaken.
Psalm 55:22

We all have burdens of some kind. It might be something we are concerned about (maybe a little more concerned than we should be) or a fear that we have. Life itself is full of ups and downs and "problems" have a way of surfacing and taking up more of our time and energy than they should. We can't get rid of our burdens by ignoring them or by running away from God. God loves us and cares for us. He wants us to give our burdens to Him. 1 Peter 5:7 says "casting all your care on Him, because He cares about you."

How do we do this? By faith and prayer we should let go and let God take our burdens. It doesn't matter if they are big or small – He will take them all. Philippians 4:6-7 says "Don't worry about anything, but in everything, through prayer and petition with thanksgiving; let your requests be made known to God. And the peace of God, which surpasses every thought, will guard your hearts and minds in Christ Jesus."

Just because we give our burdens to the Lord it does not always mean that He will remove that burden but He will sustain us, His grace and strength are enough for us when we trust Him. In 2 Corinthians 12:9 (AMP) we find this verse "But He said to me, My grace (My favor and loving-kindness and mercy) is enough for you [sufficient against any danger and enables you to bear the trouble manfully]; for *My* strength *and* power are made perfect (fulfilled and completed) *and show themselves most effective* in [your] weakness. Therefore, I will all the more gladly glory in my weaknesses *and* infirmities, that the strength *and* power of Christ (the Messiah) may rest (yes, may pitch a tent over and dwell) upon me!"

It is so easy to give God our burden and then take it back. Taking back our burden only makes things more difficult for us. When we are burdened with a problem we can get weak and be distracted from doing what we need to do. This can cause us to be less effective in our daily activities. It can also give Satan an opportunity to disrupt our lives and we don't want to allow that.

As we rely on God and trust Him with our burdens He will give us the strength we need to get through. I will never forget how my mom was by my dad's side day and night. Daddy had been very sick and in and out of the hospital for several years. The way Mama stayed with him through everything showed me how much she loved him and also how much she was trusting God. Daddy's illness was not taken away but the Lord definitely gave Mama strength. When the Lord took Daddy home He continued to give Mama strength. It doesn't mean it was easy or without tears, but God saw her through.

A year ago I had to help my mom move to an independent living facility. This was quite the job downsizing from 1200 sq. ft. and a double garage to a 700 sq. ft. apartment. Not only was this physically challenging but emotionally challenging. Mama's health has declined over the past year and it is difficult to deal with. I know this is something that many people have had to deal with, but for some reason when it's personal it feels like you're the first to go through it. Being 1200 miles away I don't get to see her very often. I continue to trust the Lord for strength. Even though I don't understand a lot of what is going on I know that God is in control and that He loves my mom and me.

God loves us regardless of our situation. As we see how God works in our own lives we are then able to encourage others as they go through difficult times. "He comforts us in all our affliction, so that we may be able to comfort those who are in any kind of affliction, through the comfort we ourselves receive from God." 2 Corinthians 1:4

Debbie O'Brien has been married to her husband, Jeff, for over 25 years. She was born and raised in Memphis TN, but in 1994, she entered the ministry with her husband when he answered the call to serve in New York State as Associate Pastor at Northside Baptist Church in Liverpool, NY.

Application

Do you have burdens that need to be placed at Jesus' feet?

_____

_____

_____

Reflection: What is God saying to you?

_____

_____

_____

_____

_____

When I Am Afraid

When I am afraid, I put my trust in You.
In God, whose word I praise, in God I trust;
I shall not be afraid. What can man do to me?
Psalm 56:3-4

I woke up on a lazy Saturday in September to a text from my son Chris who is a missionary in Kenya. The text read, "We are in the mall and we are under a terrorist attack. Grenades and gunfire going off. We are all safe but in hiding. Pray." The next hours my husband and I sat glued to the television and to the cell phone, praying and hoping for a word from Chris to say that he, Jamie and the five children (ages 7 to 16) were out and safe. I sat waiting and praying, trusting and pleading, but also fighting the fear that was rising up in me as the day wore on. The words of Psalm 56:3, *"Whenever I am afraid I put my trust in You,"* was repeated over and over in my prayers. *"Whenever I am afraid I WILL put my trust in You"* (emphasis added); a choice to trust was one that I had to make moment by moment and hour by hour as the day dragged on.

Psalms 56:4 declares, *"In God, whose word I praise, in God I trust; I shall not be afraid. What can man do to me?"*

I was keenly aware of what man could do. I was watching it play out in front of me on television and the internet. Religious fanatics had taken over a mall in Nairobi where my children just happened to go to on that day at that time. These terrorists, in the name of their god, were indiscriminately killing men, women, children, and even pregnant women. Somehow the murder of innocent shoppers would be rewarded by the god they worshipped and in whose name they acted. These men were evil, an evil that was out to "kill, steal, and destroy." I was angry and fearful.

From deep within my soul this question, "What can man do to me?" was playing over and over in my mind. Truly, "if to live is Christ and to die is gain," which I claimed to believe, what could mere mortal man do? All my children serving in African know the Lord, and without a doubt, their physical deaths that day would have ushered them into glory. On the other hand, the terrorist who would die that day would be ushered into an eternity without Christ. The Lord spoke sweetly and directly to my heart: "Kathy, choose to trust, choose to trust I AM." I was reminded that even though man can kill the body, the child of God will never die. All our days are numbered before we are born, and to paraphrase the words of Jim Elliot, "we are all immortal until God takes us home." As a child of Almighty God, I could rest in the knowledge that I AM is good, everything He does is good, and He loves my children more than I am capable of understanding, for "As the heavens are higher than the earth, so are My ways higher than your ways and My thoughts than yours."

That day in September my children were numbered among the survivors, and we were all able to rejoice in the fact that God protected them and rescued them. Our daughter-in-law, Jamie, said that Proverbs 18:10 was a scripture that she clung to on that day. "The name of the Lord is a strong tower. The righteous run into it and are saved." Jamie said the Lord's name that day was flour and toilet paper because that is what they hid behind during the attack, and they ran into it and were saved. All seven walked out alive. All seven of them have a testimony to share with us and with those they are called to minister to in Kenya.

Therefore I must shout praise to my Savior "whose word I praise, in God I trust; I shall not be afraid. What can man do to me?" The question I must ask myself, would I still praise Him had He chosen to take them home that day? I don't know the answer to that yet, but hopefully, I would still praise Him. But right now I say, thank you God for saving them. Thank you God for saving me. Thank you God.

 Kathy Suel and her husband, Dale, have served in ministry for 35 years. Her husband has been the pastor at Amherst Baptist Church in Amherst, NY for 5 years.

Application

Have you experienced a similar fearful situation as Kathy described, when situations were (are) completely out of control and all you can do is trust God?

_____

_____

_____

Reflection: What is God saying to you?

_____

_____

_____

_____

_____

_____

_____

_____

A Place of Abundance

For you, O God, have tested us; you have tried us as silver is tried. You brought us into the net; you laid a crushing burden on our backs; You let men ride over our heads; we went through the fire and through the water; yet you have brought us out to a place of abundance.
Psalm 66:10-12

When my husband and I moved back to upstate New York 13 years ago to start a church in Cicero, we had no idea what we were getting into. We were seasoned veterans of ministry—my husband having served as a senior pastor in several small churches, a youth pastor in another, and as an associate pastor and Christian school administrator for 17 years in a fairly large one. We thought we had seen it all and experienced all the possible bumps in the road of ministry. And even though we were trained by the best—the North American Mission Board and Rick Warren—we were not prepared to face the tests of church planting in one of the hardest to reach regions in the United States.

Syracuse, New York and its suburbs have been used to test products for years because of the population's reluctance to embrace anything new and different. This attitude has carried over into spiritual matters, and we discovered after arriving on the field that three church plants had been started in Cicero over the previous 50 years only to die after a short time. As a result, there was no Southern Baptist Church in Cicero. But because my husband was a native of Central Square, just 7 miles north and a Syracuse University graduate, NAMB and the Baptist Convention of New York were willing to invest in us.

So, we sold our dream house in Mississippi and bought a smaller house in Cicero. Our tiny core group of nine started having Sunday worship services in a house in an adjacent neighborhood, and ever so slowly we started to outgrow the space. We moved into a dance studio where we set up on Saturday night and tore down on Sunday after worship. From there we moved to a storefront in an auto mall.

Our tiny congregation has been gathered one-by-one, ever so slowly, relationship-by-relationship, one soul at a time. Some of them took years of seed planting and watering for any kind of harvest. That is why each one has been so precious to us. They are like our family. And that is also why when any one of them chooses to walk away from the Lord, it is so painful to us. It is like experiencing losing one of our own children.

Week after week, Karl and I would plan worship services—he as the pastor, I as the worship leader, and week after week, we would be discouraged, so much so that every Monday after another depressing Sunday, we would ask God if we were done yet. And as we prayed it through, we always got the same answer: No. God "brought us into the net" and would not let us go.

Tried, tested, bearing our crushing burden, we would trudge on. Hoping, praying for a sudden break through, a day, a moment when all those seeds we had planted and kept planting would bring a big harvest. But the big harvest never came.

Per the suggestion of a Church Planting Catalyst, we invested in hosting a NASCAR Sunday and had Randy McDonald as our guest speaker. Only 70 people showed up, a few more than our usual 60, but one lady came who had never been saved, and that soul was saved. After church, Randy and my husband were sitting on our deck, and Randy asked Karl, "Why do you keep doing this?" To which Karl had no reply. All we knew was that God would not let us quit, no matter how hard it got. We "went through the fire." Our son was deployed to Iraq three times, our daughter married, has two beautiful granddaughters and lives 1500 miles away, all who were in our core group left us, yet still we stayed. We offered truth, love, and Jesus, a place to serve Christ.

We "went through the water" as we purchased an old bar to convert into a church building. Because the bar had stood empty for more than a year, we found the basement filled with murky, nasty water, the sheetrock full of mildew, rancid beer in the lines, rotten food in the freezer, and everything covered with mold. For two years we worked every week alongside mission teams who came from all over to help us, first stripping almost every wall of the 10,000 square foot building down to the concrete blocks, then rebuilding back and remodeling the entire building inside and out. It was hard; it was tough. It was painful. We made several trips to the Urgent Care for construction-related injuries.

"Yet, you have brought us out to a place of abundance." That place is Lakeshore Baptist Church, sitting one of the most beautiful, panoramic locations of Oneida Lake. By the grace and miraculous provision of God, we owe nothing on this building and 4-acre lakefront property estimated to be worth almost a million dollars.

We have gleaned a few more souls from the harvest, and the congregation of about 100 now continues to grow ever so slowly, one-by-one, relationship-by-relationship, still no big influx of people. Sure, it is still hard and tough, but God is faithful, and just when we are about to give up, He literally does the impossible.

As my husband says, "Trust and obey, and pray and stay, and there will come a day when God will make a way, and He will get the glory."

Bonnie Novak is the wife of Karl Novak, founding pastor of Lakeshore Baptist Church in Cicero, NY. They have been in the ministry for 39 years, the last 13 of them spent in Cicero.

Application

Have you ever felt overwhelmed, felt like you were being tested, or asked to do something that was too hard? Has God brought you out to abundance?

_____

_____

_____

_____

_____

_____

Reflection: What is God saying to you?

You Are All I Want!

Yet I am always with you; You hold my right hand.
You guide me with counsel, and afterwards You will take
me up in glory. Whom do I have in Heaven but you?
And I desire nothing on earth but You. My flesh and my
heart may fail, but God is the strength of my heart,
my portion forever. Those far from You certainly will
perish; You destroy all who are unfaithful to You. But as
for me, God's presence is my good. I have made the Lord
God my refuge, so I can tell about all You do.
Psalm 73:23-28

I spent much of my early adult life on the lookout for "the one"- you know- "the one" who would sweep me off my feet, pledge undying love and devotion and vow to love and cherish me- my knight in shining armor.

Then God used a book written by Lucy Swindoll _Wide My World, Narrow My Bed: Living and Loving the Single Life_ to show me what I was missing by not focusing on His love and His will for me. I gave up looking for "the one" and was totally convinced God was calling me to be an OMM for J- Old Maid Missionary for Jesus. I was going to be single for the rest of my life and serve Him wherever He sent me.

I followed His leading to seminary and met, not one, but three men who wanted to declare their undying love for me…now what? How like God! (On the flip side I also met several men who were just as convinced the only reason I was there was to obtain a husband- I set them straight in a hurry.)

I had to be in a position of total devotion to God before He could present me with the desire of my heart. It wasn't until I was so focused on Him, wanting nothing more than His approval, His will for my life and His love and undying devotion that He was able to present me with another's love.

Now that I'm getting older, I still have to be reminded constantly that God's love is the one stable, fixed foundation for life. Psychologists tell us that we are unable to love others until we love ourselves. This may be true, but doesn't go far enough. I believe we are unable to love others and accept love from others until we realize God loves us- with all of our faults, weaknesses and foibles. The Bible tells us elsewhere that we love God because He first loved us and we are to love our neighbors as we love ourselves.

There's a definite progression here- God loves us, then we love God, then we can love ourselves and others. With those who are younger, physical attraction plays a big part. But now that I am older, have gray hairs and wrinkles, I know it's not the physical attraction that forms the basis of a lasting love. It's the relationship- the commitment to another.

"You're all I want in heaven! You're all I want on earth! When my skin sags and my bones get brittle, God is rock-firm and faithful...I'm in the very presence of God- oh, how refreshing it is! I've made the Lord my home." (Psalm 73:25-28, *The Message*)

God loves me until the end of my physical life here on earth and then forever in heaven! There is absolutely nothing I can do (or not do) that will make God stop loving me! What a promise to hold on to!

Bobbie Ivy and her pastor husband, David, serve at Hope Chapel in Elmira, NY. Bobbie has been in the ministry for over 30 years. Before she was married she served as a US-2 missionary and administrative assistant to the Adirondack Baptist Association.

Application

Do you believe that God loves you and that His love doesn't depend on what you look like, what you do or what you say? It's all Him!

Reflection: What is God saying to you?

He Is Awesome

I will remember the Lord's work; yes I will remember Your ancient wonders. I will reflect on all You have done and meditate on Your actions. God, Your way is holy. What god is great like God? You are the God Who works wonders; You revealed Your strength among the peoples. With power You redeemed Your people, the descendants of Jacob and Joseph.
Psalm 77:11-15

As I begin to look at a passage to study, I pick out a few words that stand out to me. From Psalm 77, verses 11 and 12, those words are remember, ponder, and meditate. Then, how interesting to look up the definitions of these words and see how they fit into the rest of the verses.

remember: to have or keep an image or idea in your mind of (something or someone from the past) : to think of (something or someone from the past) again

ponder: to think about or consider (something) carefully

meditate: to spend time in quiet thought for religious purposes or relaxation

We have so much to remember in Scripture....an image in my mind? The Red Sea. Daniel in the Den of Lions. The Great Flood. The Burning Bush. The Battle of Jericho. Jonah and the Great Fish. Abraham's sacrifice of Isaac. Do all these memories place a vivid picture in your mind? If not, go to that passage and refresh yourself of God's love demonstrated in each of these circumstances. I'm sure you can also think of some favorite stories in God's Word that will create an image for you.

As I ponder how He has worked in my life it is difficult to think of only one circumstance. However, one particular time comes to mind when to find work my husband had to travel 250 miles away from home. He was only able to come home about every other weekend. One day when I was reading in the Psalms, chapter 37 verses 3-11 became very real to me. I decided that daily I would trust, delight, commit, and rest myself in Him and He would give me the desires of my heart. He would find a way for my husband to be home with me. Guess what? He did! Headquarters closed down the branch he was managing! He was now home with no job! But my God is faithful and loves me so much that within 6 weeks he had a job 25 miles from our home.

There is an old hymn that I would like to share with you. I can sometimes be found reading through hymnals just to soothe my soul. Just the chorus brings to me a peace that passes understanding as this writer, Samuel T. Francis, says "All I need and trust is the deep, deep love of Jesus. This hymn is titled, "O the Deep, Deep Love of Jesus".

Oh the deep, deep love of Jesus
Vast, unmeasured, boundless, free
Rolling as a mighty ocean
In its fullness over me
Underneath me, all around me
Is the current of Your love
Leading onward, leading homeward
To Your glorious rest above
Oh the deep, deep love
All I need and trust
Is the deep, deep love of Jesus

Now let's look at the word meditate….the dictionary says to spend time in quiet thought. Is that the hardest part for you? We have house phones, cell phones, TV's, computers, radios, ipods, and everything else that makes noise. But Scripture tells us in Psalm 46:10 to "Be Still and Know that I am God." Meditate. As I have meditated on these 5 verses God has blessed me with the thought again that to be in His Word is so important. He has put so much in Scripture to help us see His holiness and His power and His love.

And then as we finish reading the last 3 verses in this passage....WOW!! After spending time remembering, pondering, and meditating on the ways that He has demonstrated His love and is demonstrating His love, there is only one way that we can move towards. We must offer praise to our Almighty God. Our God Who is Holy, our God Who is great, our God Who works wonders, our God Who has shown us know His Might, and our God Who has redeemed us! Selah!

 Nadine Sochia has been a ministry wife with her husband, Tom, for most of their married life of 35 years. They have served together in the Northern New York area, on staff, in mission work, and pastor. They serve now at the Bangor Baptist Chapel in West Bangor NY.

Application

Take some time to remember what God has done for you.

Reflection: What is God saying to you?

Brought Very Low

Do not remember against us our former iniquities;
let your compassion come speedily to meet us, for we
are brought very low. Help us, O God of our salvation,
for the glory of your name; deliver us,
and atone for our sins, for your name's sake!
Psalm 79:8-9

There have been many instances in my life where I have been, as the Psalmist notes, "brought very low." I've had my moments of desperation, of crying out, of getting on my knees, of shaking my fists at the heavens; all ultimately leading me to one person, God. And in those moments, I have been so focused on getting rid of my hurt and despair; I've failed to treasure the One who can deliver me from it. At times He has simply become my Mr. Fix-It, at my beckon call to clean up all my messes, fix my screw ups and remove the difficulties of life. And once I'm out of the woods, I can go back to living in my comfortable and convenient ways. The amazing thing is that God indeed DOES come to our rescue and makes all things better, but in His time, His way and for His glory.

I remember years back, in the beginning of our marriage, Rich and I struggled financially. Our lowest point came when we were on the brink of facing eviction. It was heart wrenching coming home from work, walking those steps praying and hoping that red notice wouldn't be posted at our door. I pleaded; I wept and longed for God to remove this anguish that I had felt of feeling in over our heads with no way out. I prayed to keep our home, not remembering He was my Shelter, I longed for peace, forgetting He was my Comforter, I cried for answers, completely blind and unaware He was standing with me all along. He was always right there. Right then, I wanted him to be my Mr. Fix-It, to wipe away my troubles so I could move on with life. How selfish I was!

The Psalmist says, "help us...deliver us...atone for us..." and it's all for the glory of His name! It's all for Him. Some may think, "Wow, God sure is an ego-maniac!" But if the Bible shows us anything, it's that the Lord's track record is flawless. That even when we are in the midst of suffering, Jesus offers Himself, empowering us to get through it because he suffered ultimately and suffered well for us. Who or what else would we want to have the credit for something He has done? At the end of it all, He persistently pursues us because He loves us, and that shows off His glory.

Looking back, I couldn't wait to not have to deal with eviction notices, knocks on our door or other unexpected surprises. But today, I realize that every single time I think about those days or retell that story, I am moved beyond belief by how real God is. How when we were at the point of losing almost everything, we had it all, because we had Him.

"Lord, we thank you that your compassion comes speedily towards us and that you truly never forsake us. Help us to get out of our own way and realize you deserve all the glory and honor in our life. Help us remain patient and grant us long suffering in our troubles, because we know that our Rescuer will indeed come for us. We thank you for your endless goodness. Help us to always make it about you, Jesus. In your name we pray, amen."

 Anna Perez is a church planter's wife. She and her husband, Rich, serve at Christ Crucified Fellowship in New York City. They have been in ministry for 6 years, and at this church plant since 2011.

Application

Do you remember any times that the "brought you low."

_____

_____

Reflection: What is God saying to you?

_____

_____

_____

_____

_____

_____

_____

_____

_____

_____

_____

_____

_____

_____

Under His Wings

He will cover you with His feathers;
you will take refuge under His wings.
His faithfulness will be a protective shield.
Psalm 91:4

I grew up on a dairy farm, but in my older teen years, my dad and mom also bought a poultry farm. We had somewhere around 100 cows and 10,000 chickens. Before we had the poultry farm, however, mom had about 20 chickens and chicks. I was riding my bike one afternoon around the circle dirt driveway; my dog was running behind me. As I neared the hen house, Mortimer, my dog, barked at the chicks that were running in the pen. The mother hen started to cluck loudly, lifted her wings, and all the little chicks ran underneath them for shelter from the dog. Mortimer would not have hurt them, but they just felt safer under the wings of their mother. This verse always brings that scene back to my mind.

When I am scared, uncertain, frustrated, and in a head-spin; when life gets tough, I like to run to my Father, and feel the safety that only He can provide. Yes, I too find refuge under His wings.

Those "wings" fascinate me. It is believed that the mention of wings here in Psalm 91 references back to the cherubim's wings that surrounded the Ark of the Covenant (see Exodus 25). The cherubim were guards or attendants, and in the book of Exodus, they were found hovering, with wings outstretched, over the Ark.

In the same way, the Lord hovers over us to protect us from danger; to cover us. The root meaning of the word cover is fascinating as well. It means to fence in, to defend, to shut up, or to stretch out in order to provide a screen against something. I think I can speak for all of us that there are times when we simply need to be covered and defended. We need a screen from those who betray us, mean to harm us, ridicule us, and trap us. When no one else can help or no one else does help—God can and He will. He stretches His protection over us like cherubim's wings! What an awesome picture!

So, how about you? Do you know what it is like to plunge ahead, even though you know you do not have the strength? God can turn sorrow into joy, despair into deliverance, and bitterness into delight. He can teach us through our darkest days.

Do you have worries, and sadness? God knows, and is already working on your deliverance. You can experience refuge under God's wings. If you are still waiting for God to come through, hang on, my friends, help is on the way.

 Kathy Aubrey has been a pastor's wife for over 31 years. She serves alongside her husband, Bruce Aubrey, at Northside Baptist Church in Liverpool, NY.

Application

Write down the circumstances right now that seem to be 'taking you under.' Trust God to cover you with His wings.

_____

_____

_____

_____

_____

Reflection: What is God saying to you?

_____

_____

_____

_____

_____

_____

_____

_____

_____

_____

_____

_____

_____

God Cares

When I said, 'My foot is slipping,' Your love, O Lord, supported me. When anxiety was great within me, your consolation brought joy to my soul.
Psalm 94: 18-19

The winter of 2009, the year I turned forty brought both relief from years of endometriosis, and a time I would learn a huge lesson of God's never-ending love for me. I had undergone a partial hysterectomy and had a normal recovery and had felt my strength return. I traveled from our home in upstate NY to Nashville, Tennessee to attend a pastors' wives' conference when I started having what I thought were symptoms of a bladder infection. I called my physician and he had a prescription antibiotic ready for me when I returned home.

This started a seven-week journey of faith for me as I went to many appointments and procedures to "fix" the infection that was inside of me. I was in agony and honestly felt as if I would lose my mind before someone found and treated my problem. The intensity of my symptoms grew worse and worse until finally one day I walked into the doctor's office (where I was working as an

RN at the time) and announced to the doctor, "You have GOT to help me!" After two minutes of my explaining my symptoms, he knew it was a surgical problem. I was seen by another surgeon the next day and operated on the next. During a fifteen minute surgery my "necrotic" organ was removed, and I was on my way to recovery.

Finally, the nightmare was over, but then the questions lingered, "Why me, Lord? Why did you save me from widespread infection when others you don't? Why would you choose to leave me here, when others lose their lives?" He quietly in my soul, whispered, "Rest in Me, lean on Me, trust in Me."

As I rested and recovered for the next six weeks, I became so very frustrated at not being able to perform my usual wife and mom duties. On one particular day, when I was at the height of my frustration, I read the above verses from Psalms. I was so moved that day by His words to me, all I could utter was, "Support me, Lord, support me, Lord." An hour later it was, "I'm slipping, Lord, I'm slipping." Over and over I said these words of faith to Him.

My biggest tangible need that day was the mound of laundry piling up in our basement! I was unable to do the stairs over and over and lift the laundry, so the task had been moved to my husband's shoulders. He had so much on him, caring for our two daughters and me, that laundry had to wait.

That afternoon I received a phone call from a dear church friend who said, "Laura, I was wondering if you needed any help today. Like, would you like for me to come over and help with anything, like perhaps laundry?" When she spoke these words to me, it was as if God himself had put His arms around me and said, "I care for you, I love you, I am always here for you." Yes, I had to swallow a bit of pride, but I accepted this act of kindness from her and our family once again had clean clothes!

So, you see, dear one, God not only cares enough about us to give us eternal life in Him, but He cares enough to encourage us when we're down and out. Call out to Him in your distress; beg Him to love you in tangible ways! He will run to your side and comfort you with His love.

 Laura Drury is the pastor's wife at Calvary Baptist Church in Canton, NY. She and her husband/pastor, Brian, have served there for 17 years.

Application

Have you, like Laura, experienced a time when you had a need and God sent you the help you needed?

_____

_____

Reflection: What is God saying to you?

_____

_____

_____

_____

_____

_____

_____

_____

_____

A Psalm of Praise

Make a joyful noise unto the LORD, all ye lands.
Serve the LORD with gladness: come before his presence
with singing. Know ye that the LORD he is God: it is he
that hath made us, and not we ourselves; we are his people,
and the sheep of his pasture.
Enter into his gates with thanksgiving, and into his courts
with praise: be thankful unto him, and bless his name.
For the LORD is good; his mercy is everlasting; and his
truth endureth to all generations.
Psalm 100:1-5

As we read this passage of scripture we see that we are to make a joyful noise unto the Lord. There is to be songs on our lips, ready at all time to give Him glory. We are to thank Him at all times, in all things and for all things, whether good, bad or ugly. God wants us to reach out to Him for everything. Wow, this should cause us to look at ourselves and see how we really are.

During times as we see them today, people are searching for truth. This scripture is all about truth. It tells us that as we lift our voices in praise and thanksgiving to God and bless Him, we will see that He is good and that He is forever. The Lord does not go away and that the truth of God lasts forever to all generations that are to come.

As we meditate on these five verses think about what we are thankful for, why we are thanking God and how are we lacking in our praises to the Lord. You do not have to be an eloquent speaker, writer, singer or preacher to lift your voice in praise to the Lord. As we go day to day let others hear and see the praises to our Lord and Savior, this truth will last forever.

Beverly Flannery has been married to Michael Flannery for 33 years. They have been serving on the mission field as NAMB missionaries. They are currently serving in Western New York in the Frontier Baptist Association where they have been for 20 years.

Application

Think of circumstances when it was difficult to sing a Psalm of Praise, yet the Lord helped you, and you were able to see His goodness.

_____

_____

_____

_____

Reflection: What is God saying to you?

A Beautiful Inheritance

Your word is a lamp to my feet and a light to my path.
I have sworn and I will confirm it, that I will keep Your
righteous ordinances. I am exceedingly afflicted; Revive
me, O Lord, according to Your word. Accept the freewill
offerings of my mouth, O Lord, and teach me Your
ordinances. My life is continually in my hand, yet I do not
forget Your law. The wicked have laid a snare for me,
yet I have not gone astray from Your precepts. I have
inherited Your testimonies forever, For they are the joy of
my heart. I have inclined my heart to perform Your statutes
forever, even to the end.
Psalm 119:105-112

Thinking about what we would like to leave behind for our children and those we love becomes more important as we find ourselves getting older. Having something of value to leave to others is a mark of significance on our lives. Often we become entangled with the idea that this involves having material wealth to leave behind along with a self-exalting personal legacy. But Psalm 119:111 says, "I have inherited Your testimonies forever, for they are the joy of my heart." Looking at the incomparable value found in imparting God's Word as an inheritance for those we love, makes it very clear that this is the only inheritance that really matters.

What else could we possess or pass on that would be a continual lamp to guide our loved ones? Psalm 119:105 reminds us that, "Your word is a lamp to my feet and a light to my path." First and foremost, God's Word is what we share that may lead others to eternal life. Nothing else is of greater importance. Additionally, the Word of God will give light and direction to people we love for daily decisions, as the lamp for the small footsteps suggests. It will also illuminate the bigger path, giving godly wisdom to be used in taking steps that affect the future.

All of us who have met Jesus as our personal Savior, Lord, and intimate friend have already received this inheritance from someone who recognized the value of God's Word and the importance of giving it away. Many of us have had pastors, Sunday school teachers, Bible study leaders, parents and friends who obeyed God's command to, "Go therefore and make disciples…", Matthew 28:19a. Often these people spent hours pouring out their lives by teaching and mentoring. What a beautiful inheritance they have passed on to us!

"O accept the freewill offerings of my mouth, O Lord, And teach me Your ordinances." Psalm 119:108 is a prayer to God that He will accept the freewill offerings we speak as we tell others about Him. Every Sunday school lesson we teach, Bible study we lead, person we mentor, child or adult we witness to, prayer we pray with and for someone, song we sing in worship, and every overflow of praise and testimony that we speak is an offering to Him, showing how grateful we are for our inheritance. Let's not forget that Psalm 119:108 also says we give the offerings from our mouths. Being a godly example to others is good, but it must be accompanied by our verbal acknowledgement and witness for Him. At the same time we are passing on this Word to others, we still need to be taught His Word. When we are giving His Word out to others, we must continually be taking it in so we will not burn out and become spiritually dry or absorbed in the things of the world.

Have you received this beautiful inheritance? Are you passing on the inheritance? Nothing else is more important than being able to answer yes to these two questions. The good thing about giving the inheritance of God's Word and eternal life away is that we are able to keep it even though we give it away! Only a wonderful

God of love could make something as beautiful as this possible.

Sherri Black is the pastor's wife from New Life Community Fellowship in Pittsfield, MA. She and her husband, Jeff, originally from North Carolina, came as church planters in 1997.

Application

Take some time and consider what kind of inheritance you are leaving.

Reflection: What is God saying to you?

_____

_____

_____

_____

_____

_____

_____

_____

He is On Our Side

If the Lord had not been on our side, let Israel say,
if the Lord had not been on our side when men attacked us,
when their anger flared against us, they would have
swallowed us alive; the flood would have engulfed us, the
torrent would have swept us away. Praise be to the Lord,
Who has not let us be torn by their teeth. We have escaped
like a bird out of the fowler's snare; The snare has been
broken, and we have escaped. Our help is in the name of
the Lord, the Maker of heaven and earth.
Psalm 124

What amazing words we find in Psalm 124! These words reminded Israel that God was with them. God helped them escape from the hands of angry men and dangerous situations. It was written to help them remember where their help came from.

It was also written for us to KNOW that the maker of heaven and earth is on our side. We are told we can find help in His name. As women of faith (or followers of Christ) who also double as minister's wives, this is great news; or it should be. If we are honest with ourselves, many times we forget this good news. When trouble comes, our first thoughts are not always that God loves us and is our help.

We forget that He is on our side. We forget that He is even with us. We forget because we are too busy remembering the problems we are facing. We focus on the people attacking us, on the anger flaring against us, on the floods, torrents and raging waters around us. We fret. We worry. We immediately think things through to their illogical conclusion, such as "Will we have to leave our church, our home, and our friends?"

We forget to remember the Maker of Heaven and earth has been, is and will be on our side. He is on our side because He loves us and counts us as His friend and child. Given this special relationship, we need to think differently so we can live differently.

To begin, we must stop isolating ourselves and stop thinking we are alone. When we read the psalmist's words again, we see that God our Helper was with Israel WHEN the angry men attacked. He was there when the floods, torrents and raging waters swept over Israel. They were not alone. They were not destroyed. They were rescued. Will God do the same for us? YES! God, Emmanuel, is with us through our personal floods, torrents and raging water. Whatever our circumstances, we are not alone. We will not be destroyed. We will be rescued!

Knowing this, we must also shift our focus to the One who helped us escape the fowler's snares. How can we do this? We do this by looking at our circumstances through God's love and presence. Stop looking at God through your circumstances. The problems in your life, your marriage, your home, or your church must be looked at in a new way. View the pain, hurts, and disappointments through the prism of God's love and the knowledge of his presence, not the other way around. Your helper is with you! Because He is WITH you, you can handle the problems.

As our focus shifts to God, we will sense His presence with us. God will reveal Himself to us so we can see how He is helping us, how He is loving us and how He is saving us. Then, we will be able to walk through our circumstances differently.

I don't know about you, but when my husband is away overnight, I don't sleep very well. For some reason, his absence affects how I sleep. I don't feel as secure as I do when he is at home. I can't drift off to sleep as quickly as I usually do. I stay up late reading until I fall asleep from sheer exhaustion several hours later. Then of course, I am exhausted the next day, and I don't function as well as I should. When he returns and I sense his presence back in the house, I am able to fall asleep with no problem - usually early because I am so tired. My sense of well-being or security is back, and I can relax. I know I am not alone or totally responsible for everyone and everything in the house.

This is a small picture of how God's presence affects our lives. He is always there, and we feel safe and secure in His presence. At other times, however, we don't sense His presence or we forget He is with us. During those times, we don't feel secure or safe. We live as though we are TOTALLY alone. We try to manage our problems on our own. We work to head off the attacks, the torrents and the flooding by ourselves. We forget we have a Helper.

We don't have to live this way. We can intentionally remember that He is our Helper. We can live our lives with the security that Emmanuel is on our side. We can live in his safety knowing He is for us, not against us; knowing that our Maker, our Helper and our Rescuer is with us through it all. We can rejoice as the psalmist encouraged Israel to do. We can sing, "If the Lord had not been on our side .....!

Margaret Harvey has been a ministry wife for 30 years. She and her husband, Ted, have been at Somerset Hills Baptist Church in Basking Ridge for 15 years.

Application

What circumstances are you looking at right now that are blocking your view of how God is actually helping you?

_____

_____

Reflection: What is God saying to you?

_____

_____

_____

_____

_____

_____

_____

_____

Trust Him For Rest

Unless the LORD builds a house, its builders labor over it in vain; unless the LORD watches over a city, the watchman stays alert in vain. In vain you get up early and stay up late working hard to have enough food—yes, He gives sleep to the one He loves. Sons are indeed a heritage from the LORD, children, a reward. Like arrows in the hand of a warrior are the sons born in one's youth. Happy is the man who has filled his quiver with them. Such men will never be put to shame when they speak with their enemies at the city gate.
Psalm 127

So many times I have been admonished by this psalm. After all, Genesis 3:17 says, "Cursed is the ground because of you; In toil you will eat of it all the days of your life." Genesis 3:19 says, "By the sweat of your face you will eat bread, till you return to the ground, …" Verses 1-2 of this psalm are clear reminders of the book of Ecclesiastes and the vanity that surrounds so much of what we do in our human condition.

Yet this is meant to be a psalm, a song of praise; and at the moment we realize in our hearts that "He who keeps Israel will neither slumber nor sleep." (Psalm 121:4), and that "He gives His beloved sleep" (verse 2), a great burden is lifted, praise and thankfulness emanates from our souls, and we begin to see God's great love for us!

Interestingly, verses 3-4 quickly follow to remind us that children are a gift and a reward from God, not to be neglected in the daily toils of life. With that gift comes the opportunity and responsibility to train up our children in the way they should go (Prov. 22:6) so that they would be "like arrows in the hands of a warrior," shot straight in order that they might hit their intended target. When my children were small, I had to be reminded of this so many times, as it was easy to get caught up in the day to day activities and doldrums of life. However, God is patient with us, and He has a way of teaching us as we teach our children. 2 Peter 3:9 assures us, "The Lord is not slow in keeping his promise, as some understand slowness. Instead He is patient with you, not wanting anyone to perish, but everyone to come to repentance."

Psalm 127 not only speaks to the family and the home, but to our cities, businesses, our country, and to my husband and I as church planters. Who are we trusting to guide us? Who is our Builder? Now don't get me wrong, hard work is important. Like many of you, I was raised by parents with a strong work ethic. But are we depending on what our hard work can get us? Or are we seeking God's guidance on a daily basis for what He wants us to accomplish? Do we dare do anything without the care, protection, guidance, and love of our Heavenly Father? Proverbs 3:5-6 states, "Trust in the Lord with all your heart, and lean not on your own understanding; in all your ways acknowledge Him, and He shall direct your paths." Likewise, Philippians 4:6-7 tells us, "Be anxious for nothing, but in everything by prayer and supplication, with thanksgiving, let your requests be made known to God; and the peace of God, which surpasses all understanding, will guard your hearts and minds through Christ Jesus."

Beloved, trust Him today in EVERYTHING, and He will give you rest!

Dana Duncan serves with her pastor husband, Derek, at Living Water Church in Lagrangeville, NY. They have been church planters since 2009.

Application

Are you attempting to do something right now without the care, protection, guidance, and love of the Heavenly Father? It's time to yield, then rest.

Reflection: What is God saying to you?

111

He Loves Me. He Just Does.

*O LORD, you have examined my heart and know everything
about me. You know when I sit down or stand up. You
know my thoughts even when I'm far away. You see me
when I travel and when I rest at home. You know
everything I do. You know what I am going to say even
before I say it, LORD. You go before me and follow me. You
place your hand of blessing on my head. Such knowledge
is too wonderful for me, too great for me to understand!*
Psalm 139:1-6

When I was 10 years old, my parents divorced after
25 years of marriage, and I lived with my mom until I left
for college. One of the things that I've always struggled
with was the thought that my dad didn't want me. I
thought that if he really wanted me, he would do anything,
including staying at home and working on his marriage, in
order to be with me. The Lord has since taught me that we
are human and not like God who can love us perfectly.

I remember the Lord bringing scriptures about how
He loved me perfectly. There was nothing I could do and
nothing anyone could do to me to make Him love me less.
Psalm 139 was one of those scriptures and has always been
a favorite of mine. I love to read it out loud and hear those
words in my heart.

Out of verses 1-6, v.5 strikes me especially because He says that He touches me by placing his hand of blessing on my head. It makes me think of all the people I don't or won't touch. Our church does some service in the community, and when I accidently touch some of the people who live on the street, I think inwardly that I better go wash my hands. How much more separation must there be between me and our perfectly Holy Father. It is amazing that He wants to touch me at all.

I also thought of how He says He places His hand on my head. I place my hand on the heads of my children all the time. Sometimes I place my hand of the heads of children at church when I've gotten to know them and their parents. But, when my children begin to be disrespectful or fight with each other, I do not put my hand on their heads; maybe the neck, but not the head. And, I'm only seeing their outward behaviors. I don't see their thoughts or their heart. I don't see them everywhere they go, when they sit or stand up or travel away from home. I know that I certainly can't love them the way God does. I can only ask God to teach me and give me the strength to love them as He does.

Because I struggle to show grace and forgive others, I struggle to really believe these verses for myself. I think I try to take His hand off my head and convince Him that He's wrong to feel the way He does about me. I can leave His hand on my head when I'm having a good day, haven't yelled at my kids or husband, planned a meal for dinner, and left the house when I wanted. But, when my day isn't going so smoothly, I don't feel like He should be touching me at all. But those verses don't disappear out of my Bible when I'm having a bad day. I guess I really have to accept them as the truth. He really knows all those things about me in verses 1-4, and He still goes before me and follows me and still places His hand of blessing on my head.

Such knowledge *is* too wonderful for me. It *is* too great for me to understand. My only conclusion is that He really loves me. He made me, He wants me, and he chooses to love me whether I think I deserve it or not. Incredible!

Heather Ruth Sneed and her husband/lead pastor, Elliott, serve the Discovery Church in Rochester NY. They have been there for three years.

Application

Have you ever thought that God couldn't love you because of something you had done or did not do?

_____

_____

Reflection: What is God saying to you?

_____

_____

_____

_____

_____

_____

_____

_____

_____

God's Love in Every Situation and Circumstance

Let me hear in the morning of your steadfast love,
for in you I trust. Make me know the way I should go,
for to you I lift up my soul.
Deliver me from my enemies, O LORD! I have fled to you
for refuge. Teach me to do your will, for you are my God!
Let your good Spirit lead me on level ground!
Psalm 143:8-10

David is in a dark place when we meet him in this Psalm. "For the enemy has pursued my soul; he has crushed my life to the ground... My Spirit Fails!" (Psalm 143:3,7). David is being hunted by Saul and knows his life is in great danger. As he feels the world around him is crashing down, he stops to cry out to God for mercy.

Often we find ourselves in the same darkness in which David walked: places where our spirit is weak, our soul feels crushed, and our heart has no hope. I have walked in this weakness for several months now. No one particular circumstance has led me to this path, except the woes and cares of everyday life. Or, perhaps it has been a new sense of hunger and thirst for the Lord that has awakened the enemy to pursue my own soul.

I began this year on a journey to learn about self-discipline. My goal was to make a healthy lifestyle change each month. Some changes were to eliminate cravings such as sodas and candies, cravings that hold power in our lives, leading us to believe they are needs. One change however, became my yearlong goal to accomplish. In February, I decided to get up between 5:00 and 5:30 every morning in order to have my time with the Lord before my two small children hit the floor running. A commitment that I thought would be easy turned out to be my hardest struggle. Visitors, sickness, vacations, holidays, summer, and children waking early, anything would give me a reason to sleep longer. As the year passed and I grew better in my new habit, my hunger for the Lord deepened, but my soul felt weaker and weaker. For the first time since I had children I was steady in the Word, steady in God's presence, and steady in my weakness. It has been here that I have found this scripture to speak to my soul. It is here that I have found great joy and thankfulness for my God who strengthens me.

"Let me hear in the morning of your steadfast love," as my soul has begged for my eyes to wake each morning I have found great joy in God's love. Our God is a god who loves us when no one else cares. Our God is a god who prefers us weak and not strong. Our God is The God who I can trust. I long for nothing more than for God to show me His ways. When the enemy inside of my mind deceives me, or when my mind compares myself to others, or when I begin to lose my sense of identity in Christ, I want to lift my soul to Him. Like David who cried out that God would deliver him from his enemies, I too have placed myself at His feet. My pleas have been for the Lord to show me what He desires for me to accomplish each day, not what the world around me expects.

Though our darkness may not be as dark as David's, we can find hope in Christ, crying out to Him, showing our weakness and trusting in His strength. Like David, I have found my refuge in the love of Christ. I have learned to hold my head a little higher, trusting that Christ will teach me to do His will and that his "Good Spirit" will lead me on level ground.

 Lesley Tubbs is the wife of church planter, Nathan Tubbs. Together they started Cornerstone Church at Bay Ridge in Brooklyn NY. They have been there for two years.

Application

Have you had your own "dark days?" Have you cried out to God, and found that He led you to level ground?

_____

_____

Reflection: What is God saying to you?

_____

_____

_____

_____

_____

_____

_____

_____

_____

God's Great Love

*The LORD is gracious and compassionate; slow to anger
and great in faithful love. The LORD is good to everyone;
His compassion rests on all He has made. All You have
made will praise You, LORD; the godly will bless You.
They will speak of the glory of Your kingdom and will
declare Your might, informing all peoples of Your mighty
acts and of the glorious splendor of Your Kingdom. Your
kingdom is an everlasting kingdom; Your rule is for all
generations. The LORD is faithful in all His words and
gracious in all His actions.*
Psalm 145:8-13

I love telling others about my God story. Thirty
years ago, God put people in my path that never gave up on
telling me about Jesus' love; never gave up inviting me to
church. I praise and thank Him every day for this.

I had been in an abusive relationship. I'd tried to drown
my sadness with alcohol and drugs, and looked for love in
all the wrong places. At the time, I was the manager of a
convenience store and received a transfer to Huntsville,
Texas. There was a church, Second Baptist, less than a
quarter mile from the store. The pastor, the associate
pastor, and many members of that church lived nearby and
came into the store every day. The pastor was a regular
customer, showing up every morning to buy a newspaper.

He talked to me about Jesus and how much the Savior loves me. I heard the same story from the associate pastor and the other members of the church each day when they came into the store. I had told them I wasn't interested in their Jesus. But they never gave up.

Then they began to tell me that they had started praying for me. About six months later they invited me to a revival at their church. I told them, "If I come, will you stop bothering me with all this God and Jesus stuff?" And as they say, the rest is history!

I went the first night of the revival, and the next, and the next. And there I met my Savior, Jesus Christ, and accepted His love, grace, and forgiveness.

I was discipled by a loving, Christian woman named Theresa. She told me about a radio station in Houston that played contemporary Christian music as well as great teaching. I listened to that radio station every day; day and night. Along with the strength I found in God, it helped keep me from going back to my addictions. Since that time, Christian music has become an important part of my life. I love hearing hymns played with a full orchestra. It's majestic and praise-worthy of our Lord. The cymbals, drums, and horns ring out God's majesty and love! (Sound familiar?). I also love hymns that are played in a contemporary style; the up-beat tempos and rhythms. God's love shines through Christian music; after all, He created it! Some songs are Psalms, or other scriptures, put to music. God's words put to music. Many a person has heard a Christian song and had the meaning in the lyrics lead them to salvation. Isn't it grand!

God's love is so much more than we can imagine. Deeper, wider, higher than we can reach, yet we see, hear, and feel it every day through the sun warming us, the changing seasons, a gentle breeze, the birds singing. All creation praises His name!

God is always with us, caring for us. We can go to Him with all our burdens and He will take them from us. All we have to do is ask and give them over to Him. Oh, how He loves us!

God is always in control, even when we don't understand. He is the biggest and best thing that has ever happened to me. He is my all in all. He will never leave me. He is holy, ever-faithful. He will love me with a love everlasting. His Kingdom is eternal and I will be with Him forever! God wants all people in all nations to know Him, to accept his free gift of salvation, love, and grace through His son, Jesus Christ. So we must continue telling our God stories to others. We need to reflect Jesus in our daily walk through life. We may be the only reflection of Jesus that another will see or hear. And who knows what impact that person may have upon the world!

"Father, thank you for your love and for sending Jesus to die for my sins, so that I can be reconciled to you. Your love is more than I can comprehend. Oh, how you love us! I will love you and praise you all my days. Jesus, you are the center of my life. Jesus, you love me, this I know, for the Bible tells me so. Amen."

 Brenda Ortego and her husband, Chris, has been in the ministry together since they were married 26 years ago. They have been at the Pleasant Valley Baptist Church in Geneseo NY since 2006. Brenda's husband is the pastor there.

Application

What is your God story? How has the LORD been gracious and compassionate to you?

_____

_____

_____

Reflection: What is God saying to you?

The Straightened Path

Trust in The Lord with all your heart and do not lean on your own understanding. In all your ways acknowledge Him, and he will make straight your paths.
Proverbs 3:5-6

December 6th, I celebrated a birthday, my spiritual birthday ~ 15 years walking in new life with Christ! Proverbs 3:5-6 was quoted to me in the six years prior by friends who had my best interests at heart; friends who were by my side as my husband and I endured six l o n g years of infertility treatments, miscarriages and many other trials.

You see, I always wanted to have a houseful of children and be a stay-at-home Mom, but the dream I had dreamed of for so long just wasn't coming true. I had a pre-conceived idea of what that it looked like in my mind. Reality for starters, I met and fell in love with a man who already had three children from a previous marriage. We eventually married and as we started to plan our lives together and build a family unit, I felt with each passing month my body betraying me. After years, many doctors' appointments, failed attempts and embarrassing procedures,

I was losing hope, and then the last miscarriage ~ all hope and dreams were gone.

I couldn't live with the disappointment, discouragement, the failure of it all; I was a failure. I was angry. I was heartbroken and in the process of it all started to break relationships. To be very honest "Step Mom" was just not good enough. Just as God would have it in the depths of depression and the verge of being desperate, I called one of my closet friends. I told her "goodbye" and I will never forget the silence on the other end of the line and then she said, "Hold On. I will be right there." A short ten minutes later, Laurie and her friend Nora (she brought reinforcements) came and whisked me out of bed and for four solid hours talked with me about God's plan and about trusting Him and His great love for me. They invited me to their church (as they had many times) and I finally went. In three weeks God really got a hold of me and started to mend my brokenness. He pushed through my anger, my unbelief in His goodness, and the knowledge of His care for me started to weave a tapestry of love and trust in Him with the areas of my broken life.

I remember when God's love poured over me and when I truly realized the price the Savior paid for me. I couldn't breathe; I was so awed by His care and His love. I was brought up Catholic and was a "good church goer", but I never felt this way before. God opened my eyes to the Savior, and I was His!

When you trust in the Lord and acknowledge Him restoration happens. As I look back and ponder over the last 15 years, God has proven He is faithful and trustworthy. You see, it's all about surrender. Surrender to His perfect plan, not our pre-conceived plan. It's about God having the 'better' plan and trusting in the Savior who paid it all for you, for me. When we trust God, acknowledge Him and surrender, we may find ourselves doing something we never dreamed. We may find ourselves leading a ministry by God's grace, we may find ourselves being a "Mom" to children never conceived in our own physical body and God may place those in your life that need a positive mother figure in their lives.

Faith is about trusting the Lord and allowing Him to direct your path ~ it's a good path. Several years after all of the above, my (step) children's mom got secretly married and moved away. The children were in their teens. Then and now, it was/is my turn to continue to point them to the Savior who can mend broken hearts. Today I am called "Mom and I am called "Nana" by four blessings from above. I would have never imagined that God would be gracious, loving and fulfill my deepest desires. His path is a good path, it is the best path.

Trust and acknowledge Him even when you don't understand, He will direct your path and someday when you look back you will remember and say "Lord that was a good plan".

Cathy Meyer is the Women's Ministry and Tapestry Director at the Baptist Convention of New York. She has served in this capacity for 13 years.

Application

Has there been a time in your life, or perhaps even now, that life wasn't/isn't going quite like you had planned? How has the Lord "straightened" your path?

_____

_____

_____

_____

_____

Reflection: What is God saying to you?

Home Inspection

Every wise woman builds her house,
but a foolish one tears it down with her own hands.
Whoever lives with integrity fears the LORD,
but the one who is devious in his ways despises Him.
Proverbs 14:1-2

Have you always wanted to build a new house? I have! Oh the joy and excitement of helping my mom look over wallpaper books and samples of bathroom tiles as my parents built their dream home when I was a teenager. Now that I realize how much work that is, I am grateful for the wonderful structure in which Terry and I are presently blessed. But what kind of house am I building as I try to live a faithful life in service to the Lord? Do I build people up or tear them down?

Hebrews 3:3 states: "...the builder has more honor than the house." So who is the builder? Are we talking about the construction guy who actually built my 1925 Williamsburg Colonial center staircase home? Uh....I don't think so! In Proverbs, the wise woman is the builder. Her influence and example to those of her "house" is ultimately to point them to the Lord and to live in an honorable way.

The one who is "building" us and helping our "houses" be strong and honorable of course is God, for He is the builder of everything.

When I tackle a new project sometimes I jump right in and end up tearing something down that I could have used in a different way if I had stopped to think. The writer of Proverbs is cautioning women to be controlled and wise as we do what we do together making an impact on our 'houses" instead of how the one foolish woman tears down things with her own hands.

How are you doing at building? Want to join a construction crew to help build a better "house?"

Elizabeth Robertson is a ministry wife with 36 years of experience. She has served as a pastor's wife, a Director of Missions wife, and presently serves as the BCNY State Executive wife. Terry Robertson is her husband.

Application

What kind of builder are you? Are you building up or tearing down?

Reflection: What is God saying to you?

Trust and Obey

You will keep in perfect peace the mind that is dependent
on You, for it is trusting in You. Trust in the Lord forever
Because in Yah, the Lord, is an everlasting rock!
Isaiah 26:3-4

A definition of trust can have three explanations.

(1) confidence   (2) to have faith   (3) feel secure

It is God's great promise to all believers who will put their trust in Him, not only for salvation, but everyday living, shall be completely secure.

These 70 years of trusting in the Lord have brought happiness, joy, excitement, and fulfillment.   Little did I know that when I accepted Jesus Christ as my Savior, that my life as a farmer's wife would become a minister's wife, and to serve alongside my husband, Roger would take me across America and land us overseas.   He has provided every need ~ physical, emotional, spiritual, and financial.

An incident in my life bears this illustration of trust. As a trustee of the Carver School of Missions, Southern Seminary in Louisville, Kentucky, I was attending my first Board meeting.   On the plane, I discovered I had only five dollars in my wallet. But because someone would meet me at the airport and take me to the meeting, I was confident I would be alright. However, when we got to Louisville, the plane kept circling instead of landing. After a few minutes the pilot told us that because of a severe wind and rain storm we were going to Cincinnati, Ohio to land. Usually the airlines pay for people's transportation, but not this time. After being bused to the train station, we had to purchase our own tickets. The cost was $4.95. I had a nickel change. After I got seated I prayed, "Lord, show me what to do." The conductor passed by and I asked him how far the train station was from the hotel where I was staying, and if I could walk the distance. He told me how far it was but then said, "Don't walk it at this time of night-someone may bash you over your head." As I was looking out the rain spotted window and praying, I felt a touch on my shoulder. When I looked around, it was the conductor. He sat down beside me. He took my hand and put bills in my hand. He said, "As one traveler to another, there is enough for you to get a taxi and money for breakfast." He left after I thanked him and I never saw him again. My heart rejoiced as I experienced God providing for me in this crisis. I arrived at the meeting safe and sound.

My favorite Scripture is Proverbs 3:5-6:   Trust in the Lord will all your heart and lean not on your own understanding; in all your ways acknowledge Him and He will direct your paths.

The hymn, *Trust and Obey*, is my favorite. "There is no other way to be happy in Jesus, but to trust and obey."

Mary Knapton has been a faithful servant of God as a ministry wife for over 50 years. Presently she and her husband, Roger, are pastor and wife at Clyde Baptist Church in Clyde NY.

Application

Do you have your own story of God's provision and faithfulness to you?

_____

_____

_____

_____

_____

Reflection: What is God saying to you?

_____

_____

_____

_____

_____

_____

_____

_____

_____

_____

_____

_____

_____

_____

Many Expressions of Love

Now this is what the Lord says – the One who created you,
Jacob, and the One who formed you, Israel – Do not fear,
for I have redeemed you; I have called you by your name;
you are Mine. I will be with you when you pass through the
waters, and when you pass through the rivers, they will not
overwhelm you. You will not be scorched when you walk
through the fire, and the flame will not burn you.
Isaiah 43:1-2

"Love," the old song says, "is a many-splendored thing." And in this passage, God reassures Israel that His correction is a sign of His love, and not an indication of abandonment. He reminds His chosen people that they have a glorious future ahead. He invites them to consider that the chastening they are enduring (see Isaiah 42) is a vital part of their preparation for His deliverance and eternal blessing.

My relationship with our sons (ages 10 and 14) can perhaps serve as a model, however imperfect, of this truth. Underlying all of my interaction with our sons – whether I commend or correct – should be love. That is, I should be unconditionally committed, before God, to help both of them become who God created and desires them to be. I would hope and pray that they know and believe that I do indeed love them, no matter what form that love may take.

Understanding that love is the motive can go a long way to making correction bearable. However, no matter whether my sons trust, appreciate, or respond rightly to my motives or not, I still must persevere in love.

But no one can persevere like God can. As He dealt with the nation of Israel, so God works with individual members of His Church. Unlike my love for our boys, which is flawed by my sinful nature, words, and actions, Father God's love is perfect. The end of that love is guaranteed (Romans 8:28-39).

Therefore, no matter what the circumstances – even those resulting as a consequence of our own disobedience, we can know and believe His love (1 John 4:16). We can, in response, give Him our whole-hearted thanks and obedience. We are able to endure whatever may come because His love gives us hope!

Every day, let's determine, by God's grace, to fix our minds on the Person whose love is the source of that sure hope. He is our true love, the Lord Jesus Christ! Surely He is "preparing the best for us, and preparing us for the best."

 Patricia Kornegay has been in the role as a ministry wife for the last seventeen years as she has been serving the Lord, with her husband, Milton Kornegay, at Central Baptist Church in Syracuse, NY.

Application

How are you doing in the "no matter what the circumstances" department? Can you in response, give God your whole-hearted thanks and obedience?

_____

_____

Reflection: What is God saying to you?

_____

_____

_____

_____

_____

_____

_____

Who Doesn't Want a Gift?

The Spirit of the Sovereign Lord is on me because the Lord has anointed me to preach good news to the poor. He has sent me to bind up the brokenhearted, to proclaim freedom for the captives and release from darkness for the prisoners, to proclaim the year of the Lord's favor and the day of vengeance of our God, to comfort all who mourn, and provide for those who grieve in Zion- to bestow on them a crown of beauty instead of ashes, the oil of gladness instead of mourning, and a garment of praise instead of a spirit of despair. They will be called oaks of righteousness, a planting of the Lord for the display of his splendor.
Isaiah 61:1-3

Have you ever been given a gift that you don't want to open? Who does that? I have never been given a gift that I haven't wanted to open and examine. There is such excitement when I see a gift that someone is giving me.

In the Isaiah 61:1-3 passage, God is telling us that He is sending Jesus to us as a gift to give us happiness instead of brokenness, freedom instead of being prisoners. Jesus will comfort us and we will have no despair. This is His gift to us. In fact, not only will God through His Son Jesus, give us all of these things, but He will give us so much more. We will become like giant oaks for all to see His splendor through us.

Today my husband and I went to a wake of his childhood friend's Mother. I was shocked when I saw him. Even though he is as old as my husband he looked so much older. He looked as if he had had the weight of the world on him for all of his 60 years. I was so happy to find out that his wife believed in Jesus. The difference between this husband and wife was so visible. She was so peaceful and loving. He was so hesitant and hard. The wife asked us to pray for her husband's salvation. It struck me that here is a gift that God has given this man yet he won't open it. Why? Why would anyone choose misery instead of freedom?

I thank God that He called me first and I answered with a yes, I believe in you, Jesus. Thank you for dying on the cross for me. I know that as an oak my leaves stay on during hard times, as they stay on in the winters of our lives. These old leaves are shed after the winter and are replaced with beautiful new leaves given from God. Our difficult times are only for a season, but God is always there to give us our refuge.

If you are going through something today and this season doesn't feel comfortable. Know that it is just a season and not a lifelong event. Stop and ask God what His will is for you in this area. Does He want to give you freedom? The answer is always yes and He will relieve you of all anxiety. How He will do this is only for God to know and you to experience. Ask and you shall receive. Accept this gift with open arms.

Cindy Schalmo has been in ministry of some kind for 35 years. She is a Christian therapist/counselor as well as a pastor's wife. In 1998, her husband, Dan began pastoring in Florida, but in 2005 they returned "home" to plant Summit Church in Cazenovia NY.

Application

Cindy encouraged us to ask God what His will is in the area in which we struggle. Record your prayer to God concerning your struggle.

_____

_____

_____

_____

_____

_____

Reflection: What is God saying to you?

Be Clay. Be Molded. Be Used.

Yet Lord, You are our Father;
we are the clay, and You are our Potter;
we all are the work of Your hands.
Isaiah 64:8

You've probably been taught that when you are reading scripture and come across a 'therefore,' you need to find out what it is 'there for'... the same is true of 'yet.' In this case, it could be replaced with an 'even so' or an 'in spite of that'...

Look at verses 5-7 of Isaiah 64. It says, *we have sinned... our righteous acts are like a polluted garment* (you may recall "filthy rags")... *No one calls on Your name...* still in verse 8 it says, *Yet Lord (even so, in spite of that),* **You are our Father...You are our Potter.**

Even when we sin, He does not stop being our Father.
Even when we are impure,
He does not stop being our Potter.

When we grasp that, as our Father, God loves us and as the Potter, He is Sovereign, and we can willingly

144

submit to being *the work of His hands*. Our sin does not prevent Him nor does it (when acknowledged and repented of) disqualify us. When He is done with His work in us, we will be like Him.

Be clay. Be molded. Be used.

Be holy.

 Laura Gillette has been a ministry wife since 2003. Her husband is Scott, the Church Administrator/Associate Pastor at Amherst Baptist Church in Amherst NY.

Application

Have you ever felt like clay in the Potter's hands?

_____

_____

_____

_____

Reflection: What is God saying to you?

New Mercy

"Because of the LORD's faithful love we do not perish, for His mercies never end. They are new every morning; great is your faithfulness! I say: The LORD is my portion, therefore I will put my hope in Him."
Lamentations 3:22-24

Life is full of ups and downs. In the book of Lamentations, we find, aptly enough, the laments of the writer over the destruction of Jerusalem. In the middle of a lament, the writer is recalling his "affliction" and "homelessness" in verse 19. In verse 20, he says, "I continually remember them and have become depressed." All too often, we do the same thing. It is easy to dwell on things that have happened to us, something someone said, an action or word that hurt us. Whenever we focus our minds on these things and relive them, we become saddened and depressed. Sometimes our perspective doesn't allow us to see past the darkness and despair.

One morning when I was leaving the school where I had dropped off my kindergartner, my youngest daughter said, "Mom, is it dark out?" We were walking in the shadow of a building and she couldn't see the sunshine. As we walked around the corner, I told her, "No, baby, we are just in the shade for a minute, but that sun is shining brightly today." At that moment, it hit me, we are often like my three year old daughter, we see only the shadow, or the shade that we have to walk in sometimes. We can't see around the next bend to where God has beautiful sunshine waiting for us.

Thankfully, the writer in Lamentations doesn't stop in the shade either. He says, "Yet I call this to mind, and therefore I have hope" in verse 21. If we only remember the sadness of things that are past, a cruel word spoken by another, a past that is unpleasant, a difficult situation that didn't go well, then we will settle into that depression, but the writer tells us to have hope in something and some One else. In verses 22-24, we see where our hope comes from: ""Because of the LORD's faithful love we do not perish, for His mercies never end. They are new every morning; great is your faithfulness! I say: The LORD is my portion, therefore I will put my hope in Him." God loves us. He doesn't just put up with us, tolerate us, or like us. He LOVES us, faithfully and without end. And the result of His faithful love is mercy. Mercy that doesn't end. Mercy that shows up every morning like freshly fallen snow covering the dirt and the mud and the mess from last night and making everything beautiful in His eyes. Think of new things: a sunrise, a flower budding in the spring, a healthy, beautiful newborn baby. The Lord's mercies are like these things, fresh and new, beautiful and encouraging. It is almost impossible to look at these things and not smile at the beauty and innocence of them.

One Sunday at church we were singing a song whose lyrics are, "He loves us, oh how he loves us." It had been a particularly rough week for me as I had learned that Friday that a student I taught the year before had committed suicide. He was only eighteen and my heart was breaking for his family, his friends, and for his life that had so much potential, yet he wasn't able to see past what was going on in the moment and realize the plans God had for him. As my eyes filled with tears, I struggled to sing the words that echoed in my heart, "God loves us." On the good days and on the bad days, He loves me. When my world is crashing in all around me, He loves me. When it feels like my heart is breaking, He loves me. When horrible things happen and I have no words to say, He loves me. When the sun is shining, He loves me. When all I can do is cry out to Him,

He loves me. When the shadows feel like they are smothering me, HE LOVES ME! In Psalm 73:26, it says "My flesh and my heart may fail, but God is the strength of my heart, my portion forever." God strengthens us when we don't have strength on our own. When our physical, emotional, mental, and spiritual strength is tested to the breaking point and fails us, God provides the strength we need to keep going. He does that because of His love for us, and as a result of His strength, we can put our hope in Him just as the writer says in verse 24. Because God loves us, there is hope! Because God loves us, we can see past the affliction, depression, sadness, sorrow, drudgery, and struggles of life and we can hope for so much more. His unending mercies and His faithful love don't just keep us from dying and drowning in sorrow, they do much more. They give us hope. Hope for tomorrow, hope for the future, hope that allows us to be able to get back up and go back out to face someone who said or did something hurtful, hope to say, I don't know what is going on, but my God does and He loves me!

So no matter how dark and dreary this moment may seem, remember, our God loves us and His mercies are fresh and new waiting to greet us each morning, no matter how dark the night may have been. When you are down, call on Him and let his mercies and love for you sustain you. He delights in this, because He loves you!

 Rebekah Brinkman is a former missionary to East Asia. In 2012, God called her and her husband to move to the Adirondacks. Her husband of nine years, Jeremiah, is the pastor of Lake Champlain Bible Fellowship in Port Henry and a church planter in Elizabethtown.

Application

What new mercies have you experienced?

_____

_____

_____

_____

_____

_____

Reflection: What is God saying to you?

God's Love Even in the Dark

"I will stand at my watch and station myself on the ramparts; I will look to see what he will say to me, and what answer I am to give to this complaint. Then the Lord replied: 'Write down the revelation and make it plain on tablets so that a herald may run with it. For the revelation awaits an appointed time; it speaks to the end and will not prove false. Though it linger, wait for it; it will certainly come and will not delay.'"
Habakkuk 2:1-3

Have you ever been to a city with "ramparts" (walls all around)? Perhaps a Revolutionary War fort on the East Coast? Or, an army outpost in the Mid-West or Western part of the US? Or even a "walled city" somewhere in Europe or Asia? Or, an African fortress city? Almost anywhere in the world you can find "ramparts" that human beings have built to protect themselves from danger and evil.

As you meditate on this passage, think about what "ramparts" you have built around your life to keep out danger. A sufficient bank account? Possessions? Children and family? A stellar career? Recently in a Bible Study in New York City, the teacher asked, "What, in your life, has been 'once and for all'? People had experienced divorce,

153

bankruptcy, and the destruction of their home and possessions (hurricane Sandy), among other things. All of the human-origin "ramparts" had weak points that could fail and fall down. The only answer that seemed to work as permanent security was God's Word. The only effective, eternal "rampart" around us and our lives has to be the Word of God.

Habakkuk recognized that God was the source of safety. Throughout this whole book of prophecy, Habakkuk's dialogue is with God. But, it is not a fake, syrupy relationship with God. Habakkuk is honest and challenging. From the "ramparts" of what he knows about God and God's sense of justice, he is free to complain about the way things are going. In verse 1 of Chapter 2, he waits to see how God will answer his complaint. For that complaint, we need to look back in chapter 1. Habakkuk is upset because evil nations who do not serve God are prospering, and his nation (Israel) is suffering. From Habakkuk's perspective, the evil people are "winning" and the righteous are "losing." Picture him, standing high on the city wall, looking out over the land, shaking his fist at God and asking, "Why?"

Think about your own perspective for a minute. Are there those who seem "evil" to you, who seem to be doing pretty well, while you and your Christian friends are not? Have you ever been injured or hurt in some awful way, even as you tried to follow God, while someone selfish and unkind has been spared. Your complaint is the same as Habakkuk's. Perhaps you have been afraid to tell God about your resentment, or simply your questions about it. Remember, if your foundation (your "rampart") is your faith in God and His power and goodness, you can ask the hard questions. You can hear from God.

Even as God, your redeemer, had an answer for Habakkuk, God has an answer for you. He tells Habakkuk (verse 2) to "write it down, so that more people can know my answer." What is that answer? "Wait. Wait for the right time." In other words, have faith in God and in His timing. In the end, He will reveal Himself in a way that answers all of your questions. But, don't give up. Keep trusting. Even if you think He is lingering too long, still wait. You'll know for sure (verses 2 and 3).

Are there prayers you have harbored in your heart that you don't think God has addressed sufficiently? Do you have any little root of bitterness because God didn't answer your prayers in the way you thought He should? Take time now to surrender them to God once again. Offer up your own impatience and limited perspective. Let

God's Spirit come in and answer your heart. Hear His voice saying, " . . . it [my answer] will not prove false. Though it linger, wait for it." What is it you are to wait for? Revelation. God making Himself known to you.

What was it Habakkuk had to wait for? Jesus. God in flesh, coming among them. None of Habakkuk's plans or expectations could have done such a great work for Israel. None of his complaints made so much difference in the light of salvation for everyone. Think about: How do the hurts you have suffered, or the complaints you may have compare to the life and death and resurrection of Christ? All of the things that happen to you (and to those who don't follow God) have a part to play in God's big plan for reconciling the world to Himself.

- Take a moment now to re-consider what you have built up around your life for protection. If it is anything less than the Sacrifice of Christ, acknowledge the temporal nature of it. Ask God to build you up in His Word and His Ways.

- Be honest with God, and pray about hurts and bitternesses that you feel He could have helped you with. Start fresh with God and have an honest and "clear eyed" prayer time. Don't think He is not aware of what your heart is feeling.

- Consider your life and your "complaints" in the light of God revealing Himself through Christ. If you can't see any hope, at least make a commitment to WAIT, and to TRUST

what God says to Habakkuk, ". . . it will certainly come and will not delay."

Susan Field has lived in Manhattan, NYC for 28 years. She is a ministry wife and missionary. Susan and her husband, Taylor, have served faithfully at East Seventh Baptist Church, Graffiti.

Application

Susan presented many questions to you. Take the time and use the space below and on the next page to consider them.

_____

_____

_____

_____

_____

Reflection: What is God saying to you?

The Yoke

*Come to Me, all of you who are weary and burdened, and I will
give you rest. All of you, take up My yoke and learn from Me,
because I am gentle and humble in heart, and you will find rest
for yourselves. For My yoke is easy and My burden is light.*
Matthew 11:28-30

In The Amplified Bible, these verses in Matthew
read this way: "Come to Me, all you who labor and are
heavy-laden and overburdened, and I will cause you to rest.
[I will ease and relieve and refresh your souls.] Take My
yoke upon you and learn of Me, for I am gentle (meek) and
humble (lowly) in heart, and you will find rest (relief and
ease and refreshment and recreation and blessed quiet) for
your souls."

We are to take *God's* yoke. This means we are to
allow Him to take the control. Let Him guide. It means to
let go of the control, surrendering, not interfering with or
trying to play the part of the Holy Spirit. We need to
cooperate with God. It's His yoke; all we need to do is
enjoy the journey. If we take control of the yoke, it is way
too heavy to carry. But with the Lord's help, we will find
REST, Relief, and Refreshment ~ blessed quiet for your
souls.

If someone had told me ten years ago that my husband, Greg, would be an ordained pastor I would have said "yea right." I thought I was the spiritual one in the family and I tried to control Greg by *telling* him what kind of husband / father and man of God he should be. I was not trusting the Holy Spirit in Greg to work in and through him. I needed to let GO and trust.

The mind is at rest when it ceases to be disturbed.

If you are not waiting on the Lord you have not entered His rest. Waiting means to continue to be productive in our walk with the Lord as we CONFIDENTLY wait for His promises to be fulfilled. So many times we are paralyzed in our fear and we can't do anything. Satan wants us paralyzed and defeated. Satan wants us paralyzed in our fear but we need to face our fears in FAITH. Fear is born from unrest.

God desires to GIVE US HIS REST.

Prayer is not work. Give God your requests and rest that you have attained this. When we rest we allow God to take over. We have victory when we have faith. Faith is believing BEFORE we see. Thank God that He is faithful and His word is true. God is working BEFORE we see the answer manifested.

Expect the unexpected.

Ask. Seek. And you will find Rest!

Michelle Cunningham has been a ministry wife for 7 years. Her husband, Greg, is the Executive Pastor at Northside Baptist Church in Liverpool NY.

Application

Are you resting in the yoke with Jesus?

_____

_____

Reflection: What is God saying to you?

_____

_____

_____

_____

_____

_____

_____

Why Are You So Afraid?

A furious squall came up, and the waves broke over the boat,
so that it was nearly swamped. Jesus was in the stern, sleeping
on a cushion. The disciples woke him and said to him, 'Teacher,
don't you care if we drown? 'He got up, rebuked the wind and
said to the waves, 'Quiet! Be still!' Then the wind died down
and it was completely calm. He said to his disciples,
'Why are you so afraid? Do you still have no faith?'"
Mark 4:37-40

It was the Fall of 1995 and I dreamt 'I died today.' The alarm was set for 5:45 a.m. and it was time to get up and get ready for work. My heart was racing as I awoke from my dream, there were no lingering details only a realization that my life would end on that very day. Feeling a bit paralyzed I began to wonder how it might happen? (...would I actually make it out the door or down the highway...would the busy street in front of my office where the busses cross be the place I would have a fatal accident?) I lay in the dark and turn my thoughts to God, could this be a message from you? ...God used dreams to speak to people in the scriptures so it seemed plausible that He could also use a dream to speak to me. I stared at the clock and hesitated to get out of bed. The simple act of 'getting out of bed' required me to muster up courage. I felt apprehensive. Do you *really* love me? Does 'love' mean I can be smack in the center of your will and at the appointed place of a dreaded reality? I wrestled my way through and with 90% trust, and 10% reluctance and got out of bed. Trust mingling with reluctance - is it really trust at all? My misgivings really troubled me and resulted in a long cautious ride to work. Across every traffic light and intersection I chased away the nagging thoughts about my dream, praying - but still feeling unsettled. I questioned God and began to question His love for me.

I made it in to work that day and for the moment felt a huge sense of relief, there was no choking on my breakfast, no falling down the stairs, no car accident or incident - instead I was safe and sound sitting at my desk sipping hot tea and sorting through my days work. It was business as usual and I was working into the late morning when my husband John called. I was comforted to hear his voice. As we exchanged small talk I hesitated to tell him about my crazy morning – but never expected what came next when I heard him whisper with uncertainty "...Last night I had the strangest dream that you died." SILENCE

If I had my teacup in my hand this would have been the moment it dropped and shattered on my desk wreaking havoc everywhere! Truth is, *both* John and I dreamt I died the same night- and it scared the wits out of me! I worked the rest of that day in the office and wrestled moment by moment with fear. Sweaty palms, heart racing, I drove home and darted through the door as if I had crossed a finish line and was physically exhausted. Faith mingled with fear left me tossed to and fro, going through the motions of life while wrestling with doubt and fear and questioning God's love, I had never before felt so alone as I had drifted off to sleep that night.

Early the next morning, I had been reading in Mark and continued in chapter 4 (see the verses under the title). Jesus words to His disciples in Mark 4 rang clear to my restless heart. Christ was calling me to walk by faith but the furious squall that came up out of nowhere in my life had nearly swamped me. *"Quiet!* Be still!" ..."*Why are you so afraid?* Do you still have no faith?" Jesus words spoke this truth to me: He is in charge. Even when my trust had waivered and I questioned His love, I sensed His presence speaking to my circumstances, He was right there. My anxious fears came under submission to Christ and I found rest in the comfort of my *Savior*: He is in charge, I will trust Him by faith, I will not be afraid, He is with me.

Where does your faith go when fear makes a grand entrance in your life? Everyday holds the potential to test the boundaries of our faith walk. Even as the wife of a pastor, I humbly submit that I am often in need of a rescue. The scriptures came alive to me that day and Christ brought me deliverance with His spoken truth – *what lavish love, my heart was set free by this truth- Jesus was with me in the storm!* David spoke in Psalm 119:92 about the healing of His wise counsel for the freedom of our hearts, "If your law had not been my delight, I would have perished in my affliction." ...and on that last note my heart sings, 'love so amazing, so divine, demands my life, my soul, my all!"

 Danielle Mulligan has been in the ministry since 1993. She serves alongside her husband, John, who is pastor of Open Arms Church in Rotterdam, NY and has been since its beginning days.

Application

What storms are circling you? What fears needs to be brought under His submission?

_____

_____

Reflection: What is God saying to you?

Confessions of a Pastor's Wife: Doubting God's Love

*"Can anything ever separate us from Christ's love?
Does it mean he no longer loves us if we have trouble or
calamity, or are persecuted, or hungry, or destitute, or in
danger, or threatened with death? No, despite all these things,
overwhelming victory is ours through Christ, who loved us. And
I am convinced that nothing can ever separate us from God's
love. Neither death nor life, neither angels nor demons, neither
our fears for today nor our worries about tomorrow—not even
the powers of hell can separate us from God's love. No power in
the sky above or in the earth below—indeed, nothing in all
creation will ever be able to separate us from the love of God
that is revealed in Christ Jesus our Lord."*
Romans 8:35, 37-39

Have you ever experienced something bad? I mean, really bad. Life changing, earth shaking bad? We all have…..or we're going to. Bad things happen to everyone. The reality is we live in a fallen world full of disease, death, and sin. (Yeah, real bright post, huh?) Does that mean God doesn't love us? Well, the Christian teacher in me says no. Absolutely not. But, my human heart has screamed otherwise.

In 2001, I experienced not one, but two miscarriages. The first one shocked me, but I recovered well and chalked it up to "these things happen." A few months later, I had a second miscarriage, though, that rocked my world. I couldn't believe it. I couldn't wrap my brain around the fact that God was not allowing me to live the life I wanted to live – you know, married, a few kids, protected life, etc. It seemed my plan for my life and His plan were 2 different things. I began to think His hand of protection was off of my life; that He didn't care that I was hurting; that He must not love me. I mean, how could a loving God do this to me, especially when I spend my life serving and honoring Him?

So, I wallowed in self-pity. Not undeservedly, I might add. Miscarriages are much more than a physical loss, after all. I mourned quietly and without sharing with anyone what I was really feeling….not even Shawn. Why not share, you ask? Because I felt so ashamed of myself. I knew the right answers in my head: God hasn't forgotten me, He loves me, and His way is always best. But, that knowledge didn't AT ALL match what was in my heart. In fact, it was a HUGE contradiction. And, for 3 months I struggled to make sense of what I knew in my head and what I felt in my heart.

Here comes my confession: After that second miscarriage, I didn't pray or read my Bible at all for 3 months. I didn't seek after God because I was mad and hurt and confused. Most of all, I doubted God's love. In other words, something really bad happened to me, and I figured if God loved me He would have prevented it. Have you ever felt that way? What's worse is I knew I was wrong for thinking that way! My head knowledge of who God is proved it. So, I felt like God didn't love me, felt guilty for thinking that way, and suffered in silence. (I bet I was a joy to be around ;))

Finally, something prompted me to open God's Word. I figured I would give the book of Job a shot. He suffered, so maybe I could figure this whole thing out and move on with my life. I mean, life was getting miserable. Do you know what I discovered? That sometimes bad things happen to good people. That the rain falls on the just and the unjust. That this life isn't Heaven. I should expect calamity. But, God was gracious enough to give me a deeper truth, too. Here it is: **Never allow circumstances to define your understanding of God's love for you.** God's love for you was settled on the cross when He stretched out His hands and died. God loves you....desperately. Want proof? Read Romans 8:35, 37-39.

Tricia Lovejoy is our guest devotional writer. She is married Shaw Lovejoy the lead pastor of Mountain Lake Church in Cummins GA. Tricia has a blog, sharpenher.wordpress.com. She is also one of NAMB's Flourish team, a ministry for pastor's wife (flourish.me).

Application

Are you dealing with some circumstances that are rocking your world? In the midst of them, are you doubting God's love? Let me be a messenger of His grace today. Hear me say, "He loves YOU." He does. Run to Him in times of trouble. Don't turn away. If He never gave you another gift as long as you lived, the gift of His son is enough to assure you of His love. Rest in the security of that.

_____

_____

_____

_____

_____

Reflection: What is God saying to you?

We Are Princesses!

Do not be shaped by this world; instead be changed within by a new way of thinking. Then you will be able to decide what God wants for you; you will know what is good and pleasing to him and what is perfect.
Romans 12:2

Recently, while teaching a women's Bible study on Hebrews 2, we discovered that it was promising to learn how important we are to God. Learning that God created us to rule the world, we ascertained that we are God's princesses. How much fun it was for each of us to don our tiaras and imagine what it would be like to be a princess! As our discussion continued, the question arose, "If we are God's princesses and we were created to rule the world, then why does the world seem to rule us?"

In Romans 12:2 Paul emphasizes that we are to not let the world rule us. What I find encouraging about Paul's request is that he also shares with us how to implement the command. Paul not only tells us *not* to be shaped by this world, but also to *change* our way of thinking. If we investigate one verse earlier and look at Romans 12:1, we will find Paul pleading with his brothers and sisters in

Christ to change their actions. Paul pleads and begs that they begin to live their lives *only* for God. It's almost as if I can hear Paul saying, "Come on guys, please, please, please start living your lives *only* to please God." Not sure about you, but my first reaction is, "What was their problem? It's really not that difficult to please God." It was not until recently that I realized Paul was talking directly to me.

Having devoted most of my life to serving God in various ministries, it was during my most recent ministry experience where I realized I needed to live my life *only* to please God. I realized that I was a "people pleaser" and a "God pleaser." My desire is to live my life in a way that is pleasing to God, but I am also concerned with what people think. While serving I would find myself experiencing sadness, loneliness, disappointment and even hurt. Confused with my emotions, I would regularly converse with God, telling him that it was "His" ministry. My intent was to give God 100% of the ministry, and what I realized in return is that I needed to stop trying to "please" people. I was allowing them to rule me. What I needed was a new way of thinking. I needed to allow God to continue to use me, and to *only* be concerned with what pleases Him. I needed to not just live for God, but to allow God to live in and through me.

God created me to rule this world, and I am a princess! I still have my tiara from that women's study hanging in my bedroom to remind myself every morning as I wake: I am a princess of the king of the universe who loves me and wants what is best for me. It reminds me to keep my focus up and not around. There is always so much happening around me that distracts me from what God purposes for my life. Every day I need to focus on being joyful, praying continually and giving thanks no matter what happens (1 Thess. 5:16-18). By keeping my eyes focused upward, I rely on God's power working in and through me, and I will experience more than I could ever imagine (Eph. 3:20).

My dear sisters, God created you to rule this world, and you are princesses of the king of the universe who loves you and wants the best for you. I encourage you today to *only* be concerned with what pleases God, put on your tiara, allow God to work through you and experience more than you could ever imagine.

Ala Ladd has been a ministry wife for 20 years. Her husband, Scott, is a professor at Davis College. Ala has a ministry to women and is a health coach.

Application

Do you need a new way of thinking? Are you still trying to please others?

_____

_____

Reflection: What is God saying to you?

_____

_____

_____

_____

_____

_____

_____

_____

_____

Love with Immeasurable Dimensions

...and that the Messiah may dwell in your hearts through faith. I pray that you being rooted and firmly established in love may be able to comprehend with all the saints what is the length and width, height and depth of God's love, and to know the Messiah's love that surpasses knowledge, so you may be filled with all the fullness of God.
Ephesians 3:17-19

In 1957 I married the love of my life. At this writing we have been married fifty-six years. I knew when I married "my man" that I would be a "preacher's" wife. This is not the case with some. Our life together has been an adventure. My husband has been a pastor, a Director of Associational Missions, a staff member at the Home Mission Board, SBC and the Executive Director of a state convention. It was never hard for me to move. I looked at the adventure and what was on the horizon for our new ministry.

We were still in college when we married. Most of my wardrobe was school clothes and a couple of nicer dresses that I had for church. I had one pair of red high heel shoes. When we were called to our first church, I wanted to look nice and found that those red high heel shoes would go with just about anything I decided to wear that day. They had to!

Having been in the field of education for 27 years, I am well aware of how kids view the real world. Our three sons were normal, typical boys. When our oldest son was in first grade, his class was telling about their dad's work. He told the class that his dad worked on cars. His teacher corrected him by saying, "Alan, your dad is the pastor of the Baptist Church." Alan's response was, "Well he preaches on Sunday but every time we get ready to go somewhere he has to work on the car." One morning we were ready for church, got to the car and I looked down at our teenager's shoes. He was dressed in his suit and tie but had the most worn our pair of tennis shoes on that he could find. We laughed at his choice but recommended that he change his shoes. He did! Shortly after moving to Atlanta, we had one of their famous "ice storms." My husband was in California for the Home Mission Board. On Sunday morning I got a call from our deacon saying that we were canceling services because of the ice. I just let everyone sleep. About ten o'clock our youngest son got up and was a little bit puzzled…were we going to church? I explained why we were not leaving the house that morning and after a little thought he looked at me and said in a rather concerned voice, "Are we going to have to do extra?" I could see the wheels turning in his little mind…a Saturday at church to make up for the Sunday missed.

In 1991 I was diagnosed with breast cancer. I felt the depth, width, height, and length of Christ's love for me as I asked Him to show me how He could be glorified and what I needed to learn from this experience. He truly touched the hem of my garment.

As a ministry wife my most memorable times with my Lord have been early in the morning. I have often been awakened with a burden and an urgent need to go to my prayer room and listen to His voice as I read my Bible and prayed. I am always comforted, given direction and know that his love for me is much more that I can even imagine. My prayer time is touched with the assurance that "He is still in control of the universe" and my urgency will be cared for. My burdens are lifted.

What a blessing has been mine as I have experienced His love: love that goes beyond the depth of the bottom of the ocean; scales the height of the atmosphere; wider than the circumference of the globe and His time is immeasurable. . How important it is as ministry wives that we impart to others this immeasurable love.

Areta Graham is the second of our guest writers. She and her husband have served the Lord together all of their married life, 56 years. Her husband, Dr Jerry B Graham, formerly served as the Executive Director for the BCNY.

Application
How have you experienced the great length, width, height, and depth of God's love?

_____

_____

Reflection: What is God saying to you?

_____

_____

_____

_____

_____

_____

_____

Now to Him who is able

to do above all that we ask or think-

according to the power

that works in you-

to Him be glory in the church

and in Christ Jesus to all generations,

forever and ever. Amen.

Ephesians 3:20